T0375415

A JOURNEY OF PERSONAL AND RELATIONAL TRANSFORMATION

Experiencing the Connection and Community of Philippians

BRUCE WAYNE KNIGHT

WESTBOW
PRESS®
A DIVISION OF THOMAS NELSON
& ZONDERVAN

WestBow Press books may be ordered through booksellers or by contacting:

WestBow Press
A Division of Thomas Nelson & Zondervan
1663 Liberty Drive
Bloomington, IN 47403
www.westbowpress.com
844-714-3454

Cover Design/Interior Graphics/Art Credit: Laura Knight Beebe

ISBN: 979-8-3850-2181-9 (sc)
ISBN: 979-8-3850-2182-6 (e)

Library of Congress Control Number: 2024905571

Print information available on the last page.

WestBow Press rev. date: 4/10/2024

Contents

Dedication

I have been married for forty-two wonderful years to a woman who exhibits in high capacity the qualities of the Proverbs 31 Woman. It has been my grateful privilege and blessing to be in relationship with Kathryn (Kitty) Elise Knight. She has been there for me as my best friend, confidante, emotionally intimate partner, lover, co-parent for our two awesome daughters, and co-pilgrim in our spiritual journey with Christ. She has walked with me in my adventures, been supportive in the difficult times, been patient when I have had visions that seemed to be too farfetched to become realities.

This book is one of those "far-fetched" visions. It has been a journey since 1985 as a Church Planter and Pastor. That is when I started this writing journey through a series of messages on Philippians, the warmest letter in the New Testament. Pieces were added in my graduate program. Other key aspects were blended in during my practice as a therapist. Now the final practical paths have been added into the trek. My wife has been a significant encouragement all along the way in the major themes of my journey and in the writing of this book. Kitty, I love you and am forever grateful for all that you mean to me and for your support along the way.

Preface

I have, literally, in some form or another, been working on this since 1985, even though at that time I was only a pastor preparing sermons. I did a series through the warmest letter Paul ever wrote, his letter to the Philippians.

Years went by. I entered a graduate program for becoming a therapist in 2012. Due to the inspiration I received in a number of my classes, especially the ones on Spiritual Formation, I began to merge what I was learning with my series in Philippians. In addition to that, being passionate about group, I was facilitating a men's group for sex addiction recovery and attachment repair. All these influences came together moving me to continue this journey personally and relationally through my graduate program. I completed the program and launched into the therapy world.

Fast forward to 2023, I have now had 10 years of clinical experience and feel very strongly that now is the time to finalize this journey into: A Journey of Personal and Relational Transformation: Experiencing the Connection and Community of Philippians. It is meant to be an individual journey of spiritual formation and a transforming group experience over the space of 12 weeks. In addition, it is an immersion into an attachment based, emotionally focused therapy infused, journey of spiritual formation through the Letter to the Philippians.

Celebrate God's good grace with me!! I am so excited I could dance!! This experiential workbook comes at the culmination of almost 40 years of journeying with God, significant others, and my own internal attempts at staying in stride with Christ. It is my ultimate desire to make it contagious and "infect" as many as possible. Knowing Christ and being known fully by Him has been the most exhilarating and eternally meaningful part of my existence.

Please enjoy and allow it to challenge, enrich, and motivate you on your journey of personal and relational transformation.

Grace,
Bruce Wayne Knight

Introduction

Why would I be interested in another Bible study?

Well, if you are thinking of an activity where everyone comes, having quickly skimmed over a lesson right before getting to the group? No, that is not what this is. If you are thinking about an activity where everyone shows up and opens their Bibles, books, workbooks with no prior investment and everyone gives their "educated" opinion, then, no, that is not what this is. If you are thinking that this is coming to hear a mini sermon that only the group leader prepared for and you are a listener, then, no, this is not that. This is also not about stuffing our brains with a lot of Bible facts and figures to impress our friends with how much Bible knowledge we have. That completely misses the point of why God gave us the word.

Before getting to what this "Saturation Experience" is about let me ask you to consider a few things. Do you ever, in your inner heart, when you are gut-level honest with yourself, feel like you are walking on a spiritual treadmill, spending a lot of energy but not really going anywhere? Do you ever feel stagnant, bored, or unmoved in your Christian life?

Do you ever feel helpless in your inability to "handle" your inner struggles? Do you wrestle with being thankful for your present life and those who are around you? How do you respond in adverse circumstances? Do you see them as pointless trials filled with frustration or as opportunities for God to show himself to be strong on your behalf? Ask yourself this.

Who or what is the core value of my life? (Jot it down here).

_____

How do I determine the core value of my life? Answer this question. Where do my time, energy, effort, attention, and money go?

_____

How would I like to see significant and sustained changes take place in these and other areas of my life? How would I like to have my spouse, children, and others who are close to me wonder what is happening to me? How would I like to win once again the heart and earn the trust of my spouse? How would I like to walk in full confidence of God's presence, power, and purpose in my life?

You can! And it is not "rocket science" as they say. No, there is no pill to take, no three simple steps to success and "poof" you're changed. I have no magic wand to wave to make it come about. However, it is only as hard as it is to set aside regular, consistent time to allow God's presence and word to permeate and saturate your mind and heart. It is only as difficult as it is to regularly share that experience with other significant people. It is only as hard as it is to create a regular action plan to incorporate what God is showing you into your lifestyle. If you will travel along this journey, especially within the context of a community of fellow journeyers (it is strongly recommended that this be done in the context of a committed group), you will experience transformation. You have God's word on that (Check these passages out. Joshua 1:8, Psalm 1:1-3, Psalm 119 [this is a long one], Romans 12:1,2, Ephesians 5:17-21, 25,26, Colossians 3:16, 2 Timothy 3:14-17, Hebrews 4;11-13, James 1:21-25).

If this personal and relational transformation experience sounds like it is for you read on!

Author's Intent and Prayerful Anticipation

It is with great joy and expectation that I offer this "Saturation Experience" opportunity to you. This transformation-oriented encounter with the word has been born out of a painful but healing experience in my life. It has also resulted in a thorough transformation in my life. That is why I am extremely thrilled about seeing you experience it. I know what God can do if we let him.

If you do not believe me, you have permission to ask my wife who watched and is watching it occur. She is very grateful that it has been occurring and is continuing to occur because I am convinced and committed to a lifelong pursuit of this. Once you have tasted the best you don't want to go back to anything else. Admittedly, I am biased. I will let you determine for yourself how valuable this journey is to you.

I can guarantee this, if you follow through on this journey of personal and relational transformation through Scripture saturation and do not see changes in the way you relate to yourself, God, your family, and others you can have your money back. Honestly, you can, but what am I really trying to say? God's Spirit, who permanently resides in us, uses God's living word to transform us as we saturate ourselves with it in practical ways. If we are following him into this experience, He will make a difference.

That is what "sanctification "is all about. He is forming us daily, internally, and externally into the image of his son. This is especially encouraging when we have made so many choices that sabotage the process. Philippians 1:6 says "Being confident in this very thing that He who has begun a good work in you will complete it until the day of Christ." Since God made you his boy or man (whichever you prefer), his woman, he began a lifelong plan of reconstruction that won't be over until Jesus comes back. So, you can resist, or you can join in with his plan. Let him have his way every day. I'll say this one thing about resisting- "God is bigger and "badder", (yeah, I know, slang, just to emphasize the point) than you ever thought you could be. But better yet, He is also the best Dad I ever had (He truly is and you can experience him that way if you just open up to him). He truly wants us to experience His best. He really does.

You may just have to accept that he has your best in mind by faith until you grow to the point of being able to claim it as His truth about you. That's ok. Hang on to our hope until you can have your own. It is my continual prayer for you that God will transform your thinking, feeling, relating, and behaving in such a way that it will take your breath away. Hey! He is God! He has a way of surprising us with His joy and blessing!

Well? If you're ready, let's take care of some guidelines for making the most out of this journey.

Introduction to the Roadmap

I call this "The Journey of Personal and Relational Transformation". It is a comprehensive and practical journey through the letter to the Philippians. The letter to the Philippians is one of Paul's warmest and most intensely relational letters. It is also relatively short and so lends itself to a thirty-day quiet time journey or a group journey of three months. The best possible way of doing this is with the combination of the two. I facilitate groups who do this. That way you have the blessing and benefit of your own personal investment within the context of an unconditionally accepting, supportive, and challenging group of fellow travelers who are headed in the same direction. It is kind of like a group of hikers hiking the Appalachian Trail together.

Learning Styles

This journey seeks to engage a variety of learning styles. This is because we all learn in different ways and if each style is accessed, it is hoped that the depth and the longevity of the impact will be greater. Therefore, part of the journey includes listening to Scripture. Part includes praying the Scripture in conjunction with listening. Another aspect which is only suggested is the part that includes physically walking at a moderate pace as you listen. Reading, memorizing, meditating, applying, and sharing the truths are also integral parts of this life transforming journey. In this way the mind, emotions, will, body, and social life will be thoroughly saturated with the truth of God's word. This way the atmosphere for life transformation in dependence on the Holy Spirit is hopefully maximized.

(Suggestion-Throughout the journey songs with a similar theme to the message of the passage are suggested to enhance your experience. These can be found in Appendix F. You can then access them in whatever way is your preference [YouTube, I-Pod, download, Spotify, Pandora, etc.] This will be done from 3 different reference points. For those who have a more conservative framework, hymns and older praise and worship songs will be suggested. For those who are more oriented to contemporary Christian music, selections from the Contemporary worship and Christian pop artists will be suggested. For those who are more inclined to be a bit more on the edge, Modern worship and Christian rock and alternative suggestions will be provided). The focus is the same. How do I maximize my intimate time with God?)

Components for the Journey

- Listen to the word – Using an electronic Bible or if you are old school, you can read out loud (the main thing here is to hear it), listen to the whole letter of Philippians at one time. I like to listen while I do my morning walking. As you listen, allow God's Spirit to "highlight" (this is a term that I use to refer to those words, phrases, concepts, sins to confess, etc., you get the idea, that God emphasizes to my heart) certain portions to use as "prayer launches" (I may pray the truth along while I am listening or stop for a moment and pray the "highlight" through and then keep listening).

- Read the word – Select the paragraph for the day (I have provided a 28-paragraph breakdown of the letter to the Philippians. The first day is for an introduction that sets the stage for what is communicated in the book and the last day is for you to collect your thoughts, reflections, plans of action, and such.) Read the selection for the day through for the first time. Also read the brief commentary provided. During this reading try to answer this question: What is the big idea? What is the point of this passage? Record your thoughts, prayers, and questions. Select a verse from this portion to memorize and/or meditated on.

- Read the selected passage again and answer the questions provided. Record.

- Read the word for the third time and respond to these two questions

  o How can I apply this truth in my life today?
  o With whom will I share this today? (We strongly suggest taking this journey with others in the context of a small group mutually taking this journey).

- Principle Application – This is one of the most important aspects of this journey. The principle is taken from the passage you have read. Turn this principle into a personal declaration statement to apply and share today. Example: Philippians 1:1-2- I am a servant of Jesus Christ who will submit myself to him and gratefully use the resources my master has provided. As an application of this truth, today, I will

- One final word –It should go without saying, however, I try not to assume anything except that I should not assume anything. No manner of mere mechanics will change lives. It is of critical importance that all that is done be done in reliance on the Holy Spirit. He is our ultimate teacher, counselor, encourager, and transformer. If you will pursue Christ with a humble, teachable, and Spirit dependent heart you can expect great things.

Day 1 - Introduction, overview, and personal goals

This day is an easy one. Take time to read over the following introduction and the "directions". If you are like me (and I know some of you are not, that's ok too), I like to have a clear sense of where I am going and how I am going to get there. These directions will help provide a clear sense of where we are going. Also, I have provided space for you to clarify for yourself what some of your expectations and goals are for this journey.

Introduction

Philippians is a letter written by the apostle Paul from prison, to the church at Philippi. It was a church at the forefront of ministering to Paul in very personal and practical ways. They gave extensively even though they had experienced a great deal of poverty. They were intimately involved in the fellowship of the gospel with Paul.

Let me clarify a concept here. It is critical. In our day "fellowship" is a word that usually implies a group of people hanging out together whether that is in a group study, doing recreational sports, or having a meal together and talking about whatever comes up. There is a small sense in which that is true in this case. However, the Greek term for fellowship is a more rigorous term. It involved an action-oriented partnership in carrying out the mission Christ gave us to proclaim the gospel to the world. Paul saw the Philippians as partners who shared in the joys, the prayers, the work, the hardships, the opposition, the suffering, the encouragement, the victories, the internal threats, etc. Hopefully, you get the point. Fellowship or partnership to Paul and the Philippians meant far more than sitting in a comfortable room, surrounded by warm people, and experiencing "fuzzies".

You will see why this concept of partnership is critical as you progress on your journey of personal and relational transformation through Philippians. The following is sort of like a MapQuest list of directions for your trip. It is both an outline of the letter as well as indicators of where each principle is located (P1, P2, etc. found at the end of each point). There will be a full list of the principles in the appendix as well as partial summary lists provided throughout the journey.

Are you ready to start the journey? Let me share one final thought. As you begin to walk through the process, try to envision Jesus walking beside you guiding your journey through the crooks, turns, valleys, and hills. I had found sometimes it was really exciting and like being lifted up into heaven. Other times it was as though the Lord got the hickory switch out and let me have it. Then there were sweet times when it felt as though Jesus had his arms around my shoulders, literally. I also experienced times when I was left speechless. You will not be unchanged.

Directions for the Journey

In leg 1 – Becoming More Authentic and Self-Aware

A key to becoming more self-aware in a healthy way and becoming more authentic is atmosphere. When there is an accepting affirming atmosphere, there is tremendous potential for personal and group growth. Each member of the group will want to foster an accepting atmosphere by modeling and sharing these four values: Absolute worth, autonomy, accurate empathy, and affirmation.

Absolute worth values each person as the person of inherent value and worth that God created him or her to be. You and I are valuable. We honor that.

A second very important aspect of acceptance is accurate empathy. This is where we set aside our preconceived notions, our own ideas, listen to the other person, and try to see from their own unique perspective. I cannot say I know exactly how you feel, but I will be with you in your experience.

Next, a critical component of genuine acceptance is recognizing that each person is autonomous. Each person has the irrevocable right and capacity of self-direction. You are your own unique person as am I and we respect that.

Finally, affirmation is the fourth aspect of acceptance. Seek and acknowledge o one another's strengths and efforts. Would you not rather be encouraged about your strengths and efforts rather than be criticized and judged by what you had not done? I affirm you by standing with you and honoring your strengths.

Partners in the gospel persevere through adversity and suffering–Chapter 1.

Partners:

1. Are called to fellowship in the gospel-v.1,2(P1)
2. Pray passionately for one another in advancing the gospel-v.3-8(P2)
3. Are confident that God will complete the work he started in his people-v6(P3)
4. Support one another passionately -v.7,8(P4)
5. Pray specifically for love that grows and is discerning-v.9-11(P5)
6. Model enduring suffering that motivates others in powerful ways-v.12-18(P6)
7. Purpose to make serving others for Christ their highest joy-v.19-26(P7)
8. Live lives worthy of the gospel of Christ-v.27-29(P8)

In leg 2 – Becoming More a Team Player

God's church is all about His glory and His purpose in the world. He sent Jesus to reveal Himself to the world and now we have that mission. Together with all the collective gifts he has given us, functioning as a well -trained orchestra or as a disciplined team, we have a much greater impact on a greater slice of the world when we are in accord.

An essential attitude to help maintain an impactful atmosphere is humility. No one person takes pre-eminence. We each have our critical roles. Whether the role is public or private, powerful or seemingly miniscule (small), they are all significant and irreplaceable from God's perspective. This leg of the journey enables you to address the essential ingredients of what is required of Christ's followers. Are you ready?

Partners in the gospel emulate the humility Christ modeled-Chapter 2. Partners:

1. Accept the challenge to walk in humility leading to unity –v.1-4(P9)
2. Model themselves after the humility of Christ-v.5-8(P10)
3. Surrender to God's will and leave promotion to God-v.6-11(P11)
4. Work out the salvation that God has worked in them-v.12-18(P12)
5. Are challenged by Timothy's example to be proven-v.19-24(P13)
6. Are challenged by Epaphroditus' example to be selfless-v.25-30(P14)

In leg 3 –Becoming More Grounded in Christ

Partners in the gospel rely solely in the righteousness of Christ-Chapter 3. Partners:

1. Place their confidence in Christ, not themselves-v.1-6(P15)
2. Value gaining Christ over everything else-v.7-8(P16)
3. Surrender the pursuit of self-righteousness for God's gift of righteousness-v.9(P17)
4. Make it their passion to know Christ experientially-v.10,11(P18)
5. Make pursuing Christ a lifelong process, not a short term project-v.12-16(P19)
6. Watch out for those who would dilute the truth-v.17-21(P20)

In leg 4 – Becoming More Wholly Connected with Others, Self, and God

Partners in the gospel build a unified team that stands-Chapter-4.

Partners:

1. Pursue unity-v.1-3(P21)
2. Live a lifestyle of joy-v.4(P22)
3. Live a meek lifestyle-v.5(P23)
4. Pray believing-v.6-7(P24)
5. Meditate on things that are virtuous-v.8-9(P25)
6. Care for one another-v.10-13(P26)
7. Share their resources with one another and rely on God -v. 14-20(P27)

Your personal notes, questions, ideas, thoughts, etc.

Personal Expectations and Goals

This is an opportunity for you to record some of your expectations and goals. These goals may include such things as: I want to see my prayer life become more consistent and personal with God. I want to be able to memorize verses that enable me to better handle adversities in everyday life. I want to develop a daily attitude of gratitude. You get the picture. You may also have questions that you are hoping this journey addresses. Record those. You may also have personal fears and doubts to resolve. Record those. This is a tool of transformation for you. No one is going to read this unless you ask them to do so. Good goals are SMART- specific, measurable, action oriented, realistic, and time limiting.

_____

_____

_____

_____

_____

_____

_____

_____

Jump on YouTube for an additional blessing. Search for "Redeemed", by Big Daddy Weave, the long version with background introduction. It lasts about 6 minutes. You'll be glad you did. If you feel like getting up and doing interpretive dancing with this, go ahead, no one is watching. Let it be a prayer to God!

Reflect on what you have heard, felt, and experienced. Record your thoughts, emotions, and insights from this experience.

_____

_____

_____

_____

_____

_____

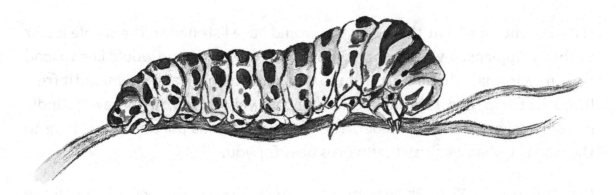

Leg 1

Becoming More Authentic and Self-Aware

Day 2

Leg 1-Becoming More Authentic and Self Aware-Chapter 1- Partners in the gospel persevere through adversity and suffering.

The overriding theme of the first chapter of Philippians and the first leg of our journey is that God has called us to persevere through adversity and suffering. Many of us like a good challenge. Some of us would rather life be safe and predictable. Some of us like life to be exciting and adventurous, but we want to be in control. The life to which God has called us in the gospel is at times any one of these, a combination, or all at one time. The hook upon which to hang your confidence is God's commitment to be with you through it. This leg of the journey includes 8 sections. The first section is:

We are called to fellowship in the gospel-v.1, 2.

Listen to the word – At this point you would have listened to the whole letter to the Philippians. If you do not have an electronic Bible and would like to load one on your smartphone you can go to You Version online and download it free. If you prefer to read it through, that is fine as well. Or you might have a Kindle or some other electronic reader. The main idea in this portion is listening to the word in whatever way that works best for you.

Read the word – Read Philippians 1:1, 2. As you read this section and all the following sections day after day try to answer this question. What is the big idea in this portion? What are my thoughts, prayers, or questions? What verse would I like to memorize/meditate on throughout the day?

The Big Idea

_____

_____

Thoughts, prayers, questions

_____

_____

Verse for memorization/meditation

_____

_____

Read brief commentary

Partners in the gospel are called to fellowship in the gospel-v.1, 2

1. <u>They are sold out to Christ</u>-v.1 Paul and Timothy called themselves "bondservants". This is a term that indicates the subject has willingly and with full knowledge made himself a lifelong servant of his master. I am my master's lifelong servant. I am his. I choose to submit myself to him in all things. I also take encouragement that as my master he has the ability to meet all my needs. All of his resources are provided for me so that I am equipped to carry out his will.

2. <u>They are set apart for a holy God</u>-v.1b – to all the saints (holy ones, those who have been set apart for God). We are separated from the world but not out of the world to be God's special redeemed people. We are separate and are to be like Him in His character. He is still working on me and you.

3. <u>They exercise spiritual leadership</u>-v.1c-with the bishops and deacons – Bishops were spiritual overseers. They provided a model as well as teaching in the way of Christ. Deacons also met spiritual qualifications but were more the servants of the overseers and addressed the temporal needs of the people. Though you may not have a formal role in your church as a spiritual leader, you are the spiritual leader of your family if you are a husband and father or if you are a single mom. If you are none of the above you can still be a leader in the way you influence others around you.

4. <u>They are motivated and energized by God</u>-v.2 – grace and peace to you... God's unmerited favor and his immeasurable peace floods our hearts and carries us along in our walk with God. He is the source of all we become and do. Our whole life, prior to faith in Christ, coming to faith in Christ, and living by faith in Christ till he returns is completely dependent on the grace of God. He reached out first to us and continues to empower us by his grace.

Read the passage the second time and respond

1. How would you describe what it means to you to be a servant of Christ?

_____

_____

2. How does it feel to realize that as your master, Christ has provided everything you will need to carry out his plan for you? How could this become an ongoing source of motivation for you?

_____

_____

_____

_____

_____

3. Read the passage the third time and respond

Principle # 1 - As a servant of Jesus Christ I will submit myself willingly to his lordship and do his will by accessing his limitless resources.

1. How will I apply this in my life today? I will apply this in my life today by

_____

_____

2. With whom will I share this today? Circle one: Spouse, friend, sibling, co-worker, peer, those I serve, small group member, random opportunity for which you have prayed (We strongly suggest that you link up with a small group which is also taking this journey, if possible).

Personal notes:

Day 3

We pray passionately for one another-v.3-8.

Listen to the word-As you listen to the precious word of God, ask him to give you a new appreciation for it and the ability to see how powerfully relevant it is where you are in your walk with him. Caution! Be careful not to let your mind wander too much. It is almost inevitable but practice reining it in. This is helpful for dealing with temptation as well.

Read the word- Read Philippians 1:3-8. At times, it helps to better understand a passage by reading in a different version. Ask your facilitator about versions

The Big Idea (Just a note is appropriate here. Part of the purpose of this part of the saturation experience is to get YOU to focus your brilliant intellect on what God is saying to YOU. Try really hard not to look ahead at the brief commentary to come up with YOUR big idea. Then when you share your insights they will truly be your insights and you will be the source of encouragement

_____

_____

_____

Thoughts, prayers, questions

_____

_____

_____

Verse for memorization/meditation

_____

Read the brief commentary – Paul shares a very important life habit of his in these verses. It is characteristic of all of his letters. The practice is that of praying for his fellow believers as well as making sure they know it. He did not do this out of a boastful spirit. He believed in the power of prayer because it links us to a powerful God and he wanted to encourage them to do the same. 1 Thessalonians 5:17 says "Pray without ceasing".

I know, I know. You are thinking, "There is no way I can do that". First, let's think about the intelligence of God. He knows you cannot close your eyes and bow your head while you're driving or any other number of things where you need your eyesight. So, this text is not about posture. Truly, prayer can become an ongoing internal conversation with God throughout the day. You are generally skilled at multitasking I would imagine. It is sort of like that. You text on your phone while in class or work. You have a quiet conversation with your friend while someone else is going over sales training. You get the idea. It's all about how we invest our time. You're probably going to say something like, "I am not there yet either". Well, we are all learning to walk closer to Christ. This passage is a great aid in developing an ongoing prayer life with God. Try using the outline on some of the characteristics of passionate praying as a tool to "beef up" your ongoing conversation with God.

1. Passionate praying is opportunistic –v. 3- "every time I think of you"
2. Passionate praying is appreciative-v.3- "I give thanks"
3. Passionate praying is joyful-v.4 – "My requests with joy"
4. Passionate praying is cooperative-v.5- "you have been my partners.
5. Passionate praying is confident-v.6-"being confident of this very thing..."
6. Passionate praying is grace based-v.7-"You share with me in this grace..."
7. Passionate praying is compassionate-v.8-"God knows how much I love you..."

Read the passage the second time and respond.

1. According to verses 3-5, why was Paul thankful for the Philippians?

   _____

   _____

   Who do you know who has been a real blessing to you recently? Do you pray regularly for them? Yes/No. Thank God for them? Yes/No. If not, why not start now? I will begin praying for the person(s) named above on this date_____. Have you told them you appreciate them?

Yes/No. Now is the time, since none of us have the promise of tomorrow. I will tell them how thankful I am for them_____.

2. Reflecting back on what you have heard of the letter to the Philippians (chapters 1-4) so far, how would you describe Paul's concept of partnership/fellowship (v.5)?

_____

_____

_____

With whom would you consider yourself in partnership/fellowship to that extent?

Read the passage the third time and respond

Principle #2 - I will develop an ongoing conversation with God that is passionate, grateful, confident, and compassionate for those he has placed in my life.

1. I will apply this in my life today by

_____

_____

_____

2. I will share this insight/blessing with those I listed above (If you did ot list anyone above why not take the time to do so now?) and also

_____

_____

_____

Spend some time implementing the Jesus Prayer- see Appendix for directions

Day 4

> We are confident that God will complete the work he started in us—v.6

Listen to the word— What have you discovered as some of your "prayer launches?" We do something enough and it becomes a habit. That is a good thing when it comes to incorporating the word into our lives. Be wise however, and don't let it just become routine. If you catch yourself praying in "automatic pilot", stop and change your focus. On the other side of that however, is that it is going to feel somewhat mechanical to listen to Philippians for 30 days. Work through that to discover the jewels God has for you in it. Diligence has its rewards.

Read the word – Philippians 1:6. Yes! This verse you have read before, but from a different focus.

The Big Idea

_____

Thoughts, prayers, questions

_____

Memorize/Meditate

_____

Read the brief commentary – Paul addresses some unity and "teamwork" issues which arose in the Philippian church (see 1:27; 2:1-4, 14-16; 4:2-3). He calls them to humility and "looking out for the interests of others". This is all based upon the example of Christ (2:5-11). But prior to that is the underlying truth which we are focused on today. This is extremely significant for us personally and those with whom we share life. He told the Philippians that he had a God-given confidence that the work God started in them, He would finish. Paul was focused on the God who was working on them and would not stop until Christ returned. He was not focused on their faults.

You may feel at times that you are hopeless and that you will never get past where you are now. Know this. Just as Paul was confident that God had not finished with the Philippians, He is not finished with you. He won't be until Jesus comes back. Has Jesus come back yet? Then He is still working on you and God completes what he starts. Is there someone in your life that you just wish God would get a hold of? He is still working on them too. Maybe that will help you be patient, let go of trying to fix them and let God work unhindered.

Read the passage the second time and respond.

1. What does the word, confident mean? Look it up if you have a commentary or can access one. Or look it up online. Then write it out here

   _____

   _____

   _____

   are in relationship? How do you think you could go about getting that confidence

   _____

   _____

   _____

2. Take some time to think back on where you used to be. Are you farther along in your walk with Christ now?_____ How about your spouse? _____ If you have progressed, that is something for which you can be thankful and have hope for the future. If you have not, maybe you know why or maybe you could ask God to show you and get feedback from some close trusted believers. What do you believe God would have you do?

   _____

   _____

   _____

Read the passage the third time and respond.

Principle #3 – I choose to stand in God-given confidence that He will complete the work He started in me and those He has placed in my life.

1. I will apply this in my life TODAY by...

_____

_____

_____

2. I will share this with my spouse (if it is feasible) and with those who are in group

_____

_____

_____

Day 5

We support one another passionately-v. 7-8

Listen to the word – Let me challenge you with something that is a little harder to do. In listening to the word, don't just listen to the words. Listen for God's Spirit to speak through God's word. You probably will not hear an audible voice, but if your heart is quiet, if you have asked God to speak to you through his word, you can be sure that he will. The question is. Am I really listening?

Read the word – Read Philippians 1:7-8. Yes, you have read this before too, but God's word is so rich. Savor the aroma of the relationship. Listen to the nearness and the tenderness in Paul's tone. Paul was a manly man. He got beaten quite a few times and kept getting back up. But he had learned from Jesus and did not believe or buy into the cultural myth that men can't be sensitive with other men and still be manly. Do you have another manly man who is this close in your life? Ladies, is there someone close in your life?

The Big Idea

_____

_____

_____

Thoughts, prayers, questions

_____

_____

_____

Memory verse/Meditation

_____

Read brief commentary – Paul had these Philippians in his heart. He was passionate about them. "I long for you all with the affection that is in Christ Jesus…" Paul had proclaimed the gospel to the Philippians and had gained many brothers and sisters in Christ. He was not merely interested in getting them a "ticket to heaven". He was also planning to be with them for the ride. This was because he knew the "ride" to heaven has many twists, turns, valleys, and hills, and many dangers. His heart was wedded to the hearts of his Philippian spiritual family. One of the problems we have in our culture when we hear affectionate language like this is that we associate it, if at all, with a romantic relationship or with immediate family. That is precisely the point. Our relationship with Christ makes us an intimate member of the same spiritual family. Each one of us should see fellow believers that way. We have an affinity (a closeness) with believers that is deep and fierce. That is just as true, if not more so than with our natural family who does not know Christ.

Read the passage again and respond

1. To what is Paul referring when he says "it is right for me to feel this way about you"? See verse 6.

_____

How important is it that we understand this truth and maintain this perspective (think this way about) with other believers?

_____ Describe a context in which you could see yourself applying this

_____

_____

_____

When was the last time you "yearned/longed" for someone? It was probably a member of the opposite sex, girlfriend, fiancée, boyfriend, wife, husband. Describe how it felt

_____

_____

_____

Who is there in your life right now that you feel very close to in a spiritual sense and would be a source of encouragement and challenge?

_____

_____

2. Can you trust them with your secrets? If not, then who?

_____

_____

Read the passage the third time and respond

Principle #4 - I will be passionately supportive of my family, my group of close believers, and those whom God puts in my life.

1. I will demonstrate my passionate support today by calling, emailing, texting, writing, or visiting (you fill in the name(s

_____
_____
_____

2. I will share my intent to do this with_____today.

Day 6

We pray specifically for a love that grows and is discerning –v.9-11.

Listen to the word – As you listen today, try to take the Eagle approach to listening. Get the larger picture, the overarching tone and major themes. In this intimate letter, Paul wrote from prison to his dear brothers and sisters.

Read the word – As you read Philippians 1:9-11, try to emphasize different phrases as you read it. If it helps, read it out-loud and do this. For example, as you begin, emphasize "AND THIS I PRAY" (NKJV), that your love may abound. This helps to emphasize that it was not just a hope, a wish, or a thought, no it was a constant prayer. Then take the next phrase and do the same.

The Big Idea

_____
_____
_____

Thoughts, prayers, questions

_____
_____
_____

Memory verse/meditation

_____

Read the brief commentary -Passionate praying is specific-v.9-11. This brief passage is rich with specific ways to grow our prayer lives. First, as you may have noticed I used the New King James Version to emphasize the first part of this verse. That was because the ESV and the NIV do not translate the phrase "and I pray" as a verb. They translate it as a noun. The problem with that is that it loses some of the power of the Greek language emphasis. The language indicates that this is not just a prayer that Paul mouths occasionally. The Greek grammar indicates that this was written in the present tense, meaning that this is a prayer that Paul continues to pray habitually, daily.

What is the intent of the prayer? What is the target for which the arrow of prayer is aimed? It is threefold: 1.That our love would abound excessively in experiential knowledge, 2. So that we will test and approve morally excellent things, 3. With the result that we will be pure and blameless until the coming of Christ. How is it that this will be accomplished in our lives? It will be accomplished by being filled with the fruits of the righteousness of Christ. What is the ultimate purpose of this prayer? It is to the glory and praise of God. It can be put in an outline form and you can make it your daily prayer like this. Lord, I pray that:

1. My love will overflow.
2. My love will grow in knowledge and discernment.
3. I will test and approve things that are truly valuable- morally excellent.
4. I will be pure and blameless.
5. I will be filled with fruits of Christ's righteousness.
6. I will bring glory and praise to God.

A huge part of our problem is that we do not feel like we are there yet. The truth is that we are all growing in our walk. We begin today where we are and put one foot in front of the other. Before you know it you will look back one day in wonder and say, "How did I get to be this far along?" You know what the answer is right? One....

Summary Prayer: Father, I confess that my prayer life is anemic (weak and sickly). I am quick to act or talk, but slow to pray. Train my heart to be aware that you desire to be involved with me intimately if I will only invite you into my space. Train my heart to walk in appreciation, confidence, and grace.

Read the passage again and respond.

1. Having read the passage and the brief commentary record here some of your reflections as these truths about prayer relate to you

   _____

   _____

   _____

2. On a scale of 1-10, 10 being no room for growth because you have arrived. 1, would be, "do what, and pray, are you kidding me?" Where would you rate yourself in your prayer life? _____. How do you feel about that? /Circle One 1. Happy 2. Sad 3. Not sure 4. Angry 5. Peaceful 6. Ashamed 7. Other ____

   _____

3. From what you know of God, how do you think God feels toward you about your prayer life (intimate conversations with God)? 1.Happy/ Satisfied 2. Sad 3. Not sure 4. Angry 5. Peaceful 6. Ashamed 7. Other

   _____

   _____

   _____

After having worked through the questions above, what is your game plan for growth in this area of your life? Here are some possible options: 1. Its ok, I don't need to do anything. 2. I know I need to grow but feel too busy to really do anything about it. 3. I plan to get a good book on prayer and work my way through it. 4. I will seek out someone whose Christian walk I respect and ask them for assistance. 5. I will become part of a small group and ask for help with my prayer walk. 6. I will share this with my spouse and seek to grow together. 7. Other

_____

_____

So, which one did you choose?

Read the passage the third time and respond.

Principle #5 – I choose to pray daily for a growing discerning decisive love filled with the fruits of Christ's righteousness to the glory of God.

1. I intend to apply this principle today by working through the 4 questions above _____ or I have a different plan that includes

   _____

   _____

2. I intend to share this with _____ today.

Day 7

We model how to endure suffering triumphantly – v.12-18.

Listen to the word –Try this today. Ask the Holy Spirit, who is our teacher, (1 John 2:20, 27) to teach you something specific for you. Then listen to the thoughts that flood your mind.

Read the word – Philippians 1:12-18 is a little longer than what we have read before and it sort of reads like a personal narrative. Try to visualize yourself being with Paul in that Roman prison. It was not anything like the ones we have today. In the midst of that mess, he wrote this letter filled with joy, hope, and love.

The Big Idea

_____

_____

_____

Thoughts, prayers, questions

_____

Memory verse/meditation

Read the brief commentary – First, let's get the context. Why was Paul in prison? He was in prison for preaching the gospel to his own countrymen. He had once been respected as one of the most notable zealous Jews, to the point of hauling Christians into prison (You can read about this on your own in Acts 8 and 9). Now he was in prison for doing the same thing they did.

Would you say that he was in adverse circumstances? That would be a kind way of putting it. But what was his perspective on his adverse circumstance? He says it this way. "What has happened to me has served to advance the gospel", both in prison as he told the guards, fellow prisoners and such, and outside of prison as other believers were emboldened to preach the gospel. It did not matter to Paul what the motivation was of those who preached the gospel. What mattered was that the name of Christ and his salvation work was magnified. More were coming to faith in Christ. Paul saw his adverse circumstances as an opportunity to advance the gospel of Christ.

Partners in the gospel motivate others by their model through suffering-v.12-18.

1. Christ-like models see the larger context of their adverse circumstances for the sake of the gospel-v.12 - "have turned out for the furtherance of the gospel".
2. Christ-like models communicate the gospel by life and words even in adverse contexts- v.13 –"become evident to the whole palace guard…"
3. Christ-like models motivate others to live boldly-v.14-… "most of the brethren have become more confident…"
4. Christ-like models discern motives for proclaiming the gospel-v.15-17
5. Christ-like models stay focused on what is most important-v.18-"in every way Christ is preached…"

Read the passage again and respond.

1. Thinking in terms of model, what kind of impact did Paul's response to his circumstances have on the people around him and those he knew on the outside?

    _____

    _____

    _____

2. What kind of impact do you think you can have on those who see how you handle adverse circumstances daily?

    _____

    _____

    _____

3. What kind of adverse circumstances are you experiencing currently?

    _____

    _____

4. How are you handling them in light of the truth of this passage?

    _____

    _____

    _____

    _____

5. How do you need to change in order to have the impact on others you desire to have?

    _____

    _____

    _____

    _____

Read the passage a third time and respond.

Principle #6 – I will see adversities as opportunities to advance the gospel through modeling Christ in my response and sharing what makes me different.

1. I will apply this truth today by seeing my adverse circumstances _____ _____as an opportunity to advance the gospel (how?)_____

   _____

   _____

2. In order to provide the greatest potential for success in dealing with adversities, I will share this with

   _____

   _____

Day 8

> We purpose to make serving others for Christ our highest joy – v.19-26

Listen to the word – By now you have gotten into some kind of rhythm hopefully. That is good and it is a challenge. The rhythm will help you become freer and more flexible. At the same time, there is a subtle possibility to ease into dead routine. One of the things I have found helpful in this area is to intentionally let some "prayer launches" go and move on to the next so that it does not become routine.

Read the word – This paragraph includes verses 19-26. As you are reading these verses, try to think of how they fit into the context of the chapter. One of my pet peeves is that so many so easily take a verse out of context because it sounds good for what "ails" them and what happens is that they take it to mean something different than what God intended. They would have known the difference if they only read the surrounding context of the verse.

The Big Idea – What was Paul's major point to these Philippian believers?

_____

_____

Thoughts, prayers, questions – What thoughts do you have as you reflect on what you have read? Over what concerns or personal needs is God leading you to pray? What questions would you like to discuss with your spouse, group, or class?

_____

_____

Memory verse/ meditation:

_____

Read the brief commentary – I would like to point out three key truths in this passage.

1. Partners are confident in the effectiveness of God's means - v.19. In this passage, Paul expresses his confidence that the prayers of God's people and the work of the Holy Spirit would be effective in his deliverance. For us it is very important to realize that God works through the prayers of his people and through the internal work of His Spirit.
2. Partners focus on Christ as the core and purpose of their lives – v.20-21 It was Paul's hope that in nothing would he be ashamed. He wanted Christ to remain the central most consuming aspect of his life whether he remained in prison or went on to be with Christ in heaven. Christ was his passion, his source of motivation, his driving force, and his reason for living.
3. Partners are committed to ministering in the here and now –v. 22-26. Paul shares openly his internal struggle over what he would prefer doing. He was facing potential execution. Then he would go to Jesus, be free from prison, the threat of death, and would no longer struggle with his sin nature. This, in fact, would be better for Paul if all he thought of was his own interests. But, he so cared for the Philippians that he was committed to remaining in prison and pouring out his life for them.

Read the passage for the second time and respond.

1. On a scale of 1-10, how would you rate your confidence in how God addresses your needs (In order for the answer to this question to benefit you, you must be completely honest. That is why we establish a safe atmosphere in our group. You have the freedom to doubt, question, get angry, etc.)? 1_____10 (10 - being absolutely confident) . Why do you suppose you rated yourself how you did?

   _____

   _____

   What would it take to raise that confidence level?

   _____

   _____

   _____

2. Fill in the blank as it really is and not how it should be. To me to live is:

   _____

   _____

   (What is your time, money, energy, emotional involvement spent doing?) How would you like to be able to answer that question? (Its ok to be completely honest here. This is for you to know about yourself

   If you did not answer as Paul did, how would you describe what you think and feel on what lies underneath that ?

   _____

   _____

3. To have someone who is willing to suffer for our benefit, right? Are you that person to somebody else? _____ Who would you say is willing to sacrifice for you?

   _____

Read the passage again and respond.

Principle # 7 – Above all else, my purpose in living is Christ, becoming who he wants me to be and doing what he wants me to do.

1. I purpose in my heart to make Jesus the core of who I am becoming today. I will seek to put him first in my personal walk, my family, my career, my church involvement, and all other areas. Please indicate your level of commitment to this principle (Underline or highlight). 1. I am committed absolutely. 2. I am committed but have some reservations. 3. I want to be committed but was burned before by some Christians and am hesitant. 4. I am just not sure yet, I need to process what that would look like in my life. 5. No, I am not yet ready to make that kind of commitment. Record in the blank provided what you think it will take to get you to commitment level #1?

   _____

   _____

   _____

   _____

   Who could you ask to work with you in getting to level #1?

   _____

   _____

2. I will share where I am in considering this commitment with my spouse/ my peer/ my leader today or sometime later this week. I will share this with my group by _____. I will share this with a close friend I trust

   _____

   _____

Day 9

We live lives worthy of the gospel of Christ –v. 27-30

Listen to the word – Do you have a favorite song? When you first hear it start to play what is the first feeling you get (If you need to do so, pull out your Feeling Wheel to identify these emotions.)? Excitement? Aggressive? Pumped Up? Anticipation? Romantic? Peaceful? Worshipful? As you begin to listen to God's word, allow him to develop a grateful anticipation for what he is about to do in you. Lord, give me a heart that is passionate to hear from you. Thank you for this opportunity to have intimate fellowship.

Read the word - Read Philippians 1:27-30. Do you know what it is for a cow to chew the cud? Part of their process in eating is to chew the grass, hay, or whatever. Then they will swallow it into their first stomach, regurgitate it and then start chewing again. This is what is called chewing the cud. Following the analogy, read a phrase or sentence, slow down to reflect on how it applies to you. Read it again focusing on different phrases as they speak to your soul. Then in the next section record what God has spoken to you.

The Big Idea

_____

_____

_____

Thoughts, prayers, questions

_____

_____

_____

Memory verse/meditation

_____

Read the brief commentary –Let me first offer a disclaimer. This passage is going to be a bit difficult for two reasons. 1. When we talk about the idea of suffering for Christ, we become a bit squeamish. 2. Our concept of "suffering" sometimes is not in sync with the Bible's idea. So, allow God to work with you.

Whenever anything is the first to come, it is significant because it sets the tone for everything else that follows. That is precisely what takes place in this passage. Verse 27 records the first imperative in the letter to the Philippians. This is the first command Paul gives. "Live lives worthy of the gospel". The ESV has it this way, "Let your manner of life be worthy of the gospel"

In Paul's introduction (Chapter1), he models what living life worthy of the gospel would look like. He introduces himself as a servant of Christ, not an apostle. He is humble. He demonstrates a grateful attitude. He models a passionate prayer life. He affirms his brothers and sisters by expressing his confidence in God's ability to complete His work in them. He models how to suffer for Christ. Then he throws down the challenge. You live lives worthy of the gospel. Follow my lead.

Paul also spells out specifically what it means for the Philippians to live worthy of the gospel. He paints the picture of a team in competition with one purpose, one spirit, side by side striving for the faith of the gospel. There will be opposition, so, it is imperative to work together closely. To win this competition, it takes everyone working together as one unit. Do you remember the movie, Gladiator, and the scene in the coliseum where they were about to be killed by the charioteers with arrows? Do you remember what Maximus did? He rallied his fellow slaves together "as one" and as gross underdogs to defeat the charioteers.

In verses 29-30 Paul addresses the grim reality that those who follow Christ will experience suffering. Notice, however, how Paul refers to suffering. "It has been granted to you...that you should suffer for his sake." In other words, it is a gift. Suffering for Christ is a gift. Does not that sound odd? Notice two things. This suffering is not self-inflicted. It is not because we have sinned. It is not because we live in a fallen world where bad things happen. This suffering arises upon those who are living out the gospel and proclaiming Christ.

The second thing to notice is this. Suffering is a gift to those whom God has prepared. Paul was at that place. For Pau,l living was all about Jesus. He had lost himself in Christ and viewed all that came into his life as if it came from the hand of God. He accepted his suffering and saw it as an opportunity to glorify God and advance the gospel.

Read the passage again and respond.

1. When Paul says we are to live a life worthy of the gospel, what does that look like? Let's go back to the gospels and examine the life of Jesus. How did he live? As you reflect on Jesus' life, think about the areas listed below and record your thoughts concerning what it means to live life worthy of the gospel (Take a stroll in the gospels – Mark is the shortest, 16 chapters. It is perfect for our fast- paced culture. Hint: Another approach is to use online Bible tools if that is safe for you. Yes, this one is quite a bit more challenging. It is optional, but well worth it.).

    a. Mental/thought life

    _____

    _____

    Emotional/psychological

    _____

    _____

    b. Relational/personal relationships

    _____

    _____

    _____

    Family/social

    _____

    _____

    c. Volitional/choices

    _____

    _____

    d. Spiritual

_____

_____

e. What do you see that you can apply in your life from Christ's and Paul's example

_____

_____

_____

2. After reading this portion of Scripture how would you describe your view of suffering for Christ?

_____

_____

Have you experienced this kind of suffering? Circle one Yes/No. What was it like for you? Describe it in terms of relationships, internal emotional response, and spiritual effect on your life

_____

_____

_____

_____

Read the passage for the third time and respond.

Principle #8 – By faith I accept the eventual reality that living worthy of the gospel will bring to me the gift of suffering for Christ.

1. How do you intend to apply this principle in your life this week? I will

_____

_____

2. I will share what God has taught me, the reservations I have, or the questions I have with my spouse, my group, or my accountability partners on this coming(day) _____ of this week.

Day 10 – Leg 1 - Summary of Transformation Principles

For this summary day and the for the following legs, we recommend that this be a time of extended worship utilizing your favorite worship songs and artists. Let loose and enjoy some time with God. Whether you prefer being loud and excitable or quiet and reflective or a little of both, let His Spirit lead you into it. Yes?

As you work through these principles in the form of evaluation questions allow God to reveal your heart. Reflect on these deeply and record honestly where you are. Celebrate the growth you have made. Acknowledge the areas for greater growth. Identify areas where you feel you need help from your spouse, your group, or your spiritual leader. Many intend to grow closer to Christ or to others but do not have a plan for doing so. Years later, they are still intending to grow, but have not.

You can grow in Christ beyond what you would ever think possible, but it does not happen on its own. We are not suggesting self-made growth, but simply having a plan to use the means God has provided to grow in Christ in the context of Christian community. So, after you work through the list of the first 8 principles, use the format provided or your own creation to develop your God-directed plan for growing in Christ in the areas you have identified. It is not required, but it may be helpful to use a scale of 1- 10 to locate where you think you are on each principle.

Principle #1- v.1, 2 -As a servant of Jesus Christ I will submit myself willingly to his lordship and do his will by accessing his limitless resources.

How am I thinking, feeling, and acting as a servant of Christ, submitted to Him and accessing all of my master's resources?

Principle #2 – v. 3-5-- I will develop an ongoing conversation with God for people in my life that is passionate, grateful, confident, and compassionate.

How am I developing an ongoing conversation with God that is passionate, grateful, confident, and compassionate for those he has placed in my life?

_____

_____

Principle #3 –v. 6- I choose to stand in God-given confidence that He will complete the work He started in me and key people in my life. ((0-10 scale)

How is my level of confidence growing in God's ability to complete the work He started in me, my family, and those he puts in my life?

_____

_____

Principle #4 – v. 7-8- I will be passionately supportive of my family, close believers, and others God puts in my life.

How am I doing at being passionate and compassionate for those whom God has placed in my life? Describe specific ways in which you are applying this principle

_____

_____

Principle #5 – v.9-11- I choose to pray daily for a growing, discerning, decisive love, filled with the fruits of Christ's righteousness to the glory of God.

How well am I doing praying for a love that is discerning, decisive, and filled with the righteous fruits of Christ? Am I praying that for those I love? Am I seeing the results of this prayer in my life? Describe your practices for reaching these targets

_____

_____

Principle #6 – v.12-18 - I will see adversities as opportunities to advance the gospel through modeling Christ in my response and sharing what makes me different.

How well am I doing at choosing to see adverse circumstances as opportunities to advance the gospel? Describe specific adverse circumstances you have experienced recently and how you responded differently than you normally would have in the past

_____

_____

_____

Principle #7 - v. 19-26 - Above all else, my purpose in living is Christ, becoming who he wants me to be, and doing what he wants me to do.

Describe specific ways in which Jesus is at the core of who you are becoming?

_____

_____

How is Christ being magnified in my body, thinking, feeling, choices?

_____

_____

Principle #8 – v. 27-30 - By faith I accept the eventual reality that living worthy of the gospel will bring to me the gift of suffering for Christ.

Have I come to a place in my life where I can accept suffering for Christ and the gospel as a gift from God? _____What needs to take place in my life for me to be at that point?

_____

_____

My Action Plan for Pursuing Growth in Christ (Philippians 3: 13, 14 - ¹³ Brothers, I do not consider that I have made it my own. But one thing I do: forgetting what lies behind and straining forward to what lays ahead, [14] I press on toward the goal for the prize of the upward call of God in Christ Jesus[1])

1. These are the areas of growth in my walk with Jesus. I praise him for these areas and I will celebrate these by

    _____

    _____

2. These are areas where I have seen some growth but want to see more growth. My plan for continued growth includes: SMART goals = Specific/ Measurable/Action oriented/Realistic/Time limited

    _____

    _____

3. These are areas where I feel like I am floundering and if I am truly honest with myself, I need help (We all have those areas in our lives. So, join the party). This is just a suggestion. Rather than pick many areas, why not focus on one for each category. Then, when you feel comfortable with your progress, you can always add to your growth list.

    a. I need help from my spouse/significant other in this area

        _____

    b. I need help from my group/close friends in this area

        _____

    c. I need help from my spiritual leader/elder/pastor/counselor in this area

        _____

        _____

_____

[1] *The Holy Bible: English Standard Version.* 2001 (Philippians 3:13–14). Wheaton: Standard Bible Society.

Leg 2

Becoming More a Team Player

Day 11

Leg 2 – Becoming More a Team Player-Chapter 2- Partners in the gospel emulate (model) the humility which Christ modeled.

In the second leg of the journey, you will discover one of the most humbling and awe-inspiring reasons why our Lord Jesus Christ is so wonderful. You will also be challenged to live life from a completely different perspective than our culture advocates. Although that may be true, this life is one that offers the greatest sense of true accomplishment, contentment, and soul liberation because you will be learning how to experience joy through serving. The central theme of this chapter rests in three imperatives (commands). You will find these imperatives recorded for us in chapter 2:3-5. "Count others more significant than yourselves"." Look out for the interests of others". "Let this settled mind be in you which was also in Christ".

Following these verses, Paul rehearses how Jesus did the very thing he commands of the Philippians. Christ humbled himself to come to earth, serve, and die on a cross for us. The rest of the chapter reiterates the imperatives above as Paul, Timothy, and Epaproditus are paraded before the Philippians as models. Are you ready to have your world rocked? Here is how leg two begins:

We emulate (model) the humility which Christ modeled – v.1-4

Listen to the word - As you listen to chapter two, listen especially for the themes of humility and service and how they are modeled by those listed in this chapter. Allow God to speak to your heart through this.

Read the word –Read chapter 2:1-4. Paul begins with a series of statements all beginning with the word, "if". This is a device, which the Greek language uses to emphasize a point. It could be translated better, "Since". Now read it that way. These are not wishful statements. They are affirmative statements.

The Big Idea

_____

Thoughts, prayers, questions (What personal prayer requests has the Lord prompted you to pray from this passage? What are some of your responses to these truths?)

_____

_____

_____

_____

_____

Memory verse/Meditation verse

Read the brief commentary – Do you want to know what the will of God is for your life? Many believers do and that is great. The primary way in which God reveals his will is through his word and his character. One of the primary ways his word clarifies his will is through commands. In verses 1-4 we have a clear statement of one aspect of God's will for us. Here, it is given in three commands.

1. Fulfill my joy by being likeminded (Live in unity) – v. 2 (Think of the movie, "Gladiator" as the gladiators are in Rome's arena and Maximus yells out "As one". They defeat the charioteers.)
2. Consider others more significant than yourself – v.3
3. Look out for the interests of others as well as your own – v.4

One of the most powerful aspects of this mandate is that Paul gave us a vivid picture of what it meant – Jesus, coming from heaven's glory to live in a tainted world, suffer, and die for our sin. This was the height of "looking out for the interest of others".

Read the passage again and respond.

1. This is not a call to uniformity (everyone being the same, doing the same) where everyone gives up individuality and is consumed into to the collective (like the Borg on StarTrek). We are called to real unity where "it" is not all about me. In this passage, what are identified as motivating factors for living in unity? Suggestion: The word, therefore, in the beginning, points back to what was said previously and verse one has some clues

_____

_____

_____

_____

_____

2. What factors of motivation are most appealing to you?

_____

_____

In 2:1-4, Paul seeks to persuade the Philippians with four motivating factors? What are they?

_____

_____

Think of times when you experienced each of these. What was it like? How did it make you feel (use the Feeling Wheel if needed)?

_____

_____

_____

3. How can you "consider others more significant than yourself" in practical ways beginning with your spouse, kids, and family? Think of ways you can demonstrate you value them? Your peers? Those you serve? Describe how that would look.(use more space if necessary)

_____

_____

_____

What would that look like in your group or with your friends?

_____

_____

4. How can you "look out for the interests of others" today? Make a "Things to do" list for yourself today. Brainstorm. Remember all those things you

wished you would have done or said involving others. Just write it all out. Then share it with your spouse, group, or a trusted friend. This is my to do list:

a. _____

b. _____

c. _____

d. _____

e. _____

f. _____

g. _____

h. _____

i. _____

j. _____

Read the passage the third time and respond.

Principle # 9 – Because of all that God has done for me and because of all the support he has placed around me I choose to be a humble team player and others focused.

1. What is your plan for becoming more others oriented? Describe it in detail.

   _____

   _____

2. Who do you intend to bring on your support team to help you accomplish this? List them here.

   _____

   _____

Day 12

We leave promotion to God and seek to serve – v. 5-11

Listen to the word – How precious is the word to you? Imagine yourself in a fundamentalist Muslim country where it is against the law to be a Christian and the word of God is outlawed. How would you be able to interact with God's word?

Read the word – The passage for today (2:5-11), is a classic passage on the doctrine of, what in theology is called the hypostatic union of Christ. Simply put, it is the truth of the two natures of Christ existing in one body, not mixed, fully human, and fully divine. How, you say, can that be? It is truly one of those mysteries of the faith, which causes us to bow in reverent worship. Let some of that worship happen today as you read about our wonderful Lord.

The Big Idea

_____

_____

_____

Thoughts, prayers, questions

_____

_____

_____

Meditation/memory verse:

_____

Read the brief commentary – As already mentioned, this section focuses on Christ's move from his position of glory and honor in heaven to humble himself as a servant on earth. As he obeyed the Father in fulfilling his purpose, he surrendered himself to be crucified and die in our place. Then, God raised him from the dead as victor over sin and death and exalted him to his former position in glory.

Let us not miss the impetus (point) of this whole discussion. Look once again at verse 5. This great truth of Christ's humiliation and exaltation is set in the context of the command given to the Philippians. "Let this settled mind be in you that was also in Christ". What was that settled mind? His life was consumed with humble obedience to the Father in serving and sacrificing for us. Paul felt that it was so important to impress this truth upon the Philippians that he could think of no better way than to use the example of Christ.

1. Partners are commanded to have a humble, others- oriented mindset v. 5
2. Partners are compelled by the model of Christ - v. 6-11

   a. Christ left willingly his exalted position v. 6,7
   b. Christ obeyed humbly to the death – v. 8.
   c. Christ was exalted ultimately to glory by God the Father –v. 9-11

Read the passage again and respond.

1. What is the first thing that crosses your mind when you read "Let this mind be in you that was also in Christ?"_____

   When you realize that it is a demonstration of the authenticity of your walk with Christ how do you respond to that?

   _____

   _____

2. Make a list of all the aspects of Christ's model and character that you appreciate as you read this passage. Have you told him personally how much you appreciate him? Yes / No? Why not take time now to tell him all the things you appreciate and admire about him. Make it very personal. Record those here and elsewhere if you need space.

   _____

   _____

3. What do you think, believe, feel is the biggest obstacle in your way that prevents you from living out this mindset?

_____

_____

How do you intend to address it?

_____

_____

With whom do you intend to share this step forward?

_____

Read the passage again and respond

Principle # 10/11- My settled attitude toward God and for others will be humble obedience to God's will. Like Christ, I will surrender promotion to the Father and look to him for his time and way.

1. Describe how you envision putting this principle into practice today and record your images. Maybe this would be helpful. Use Christ's 3 step process as a gauge. 1. Willingly surrender your position or expectation. 2. Decide daily to practice humble obedience to Him as reflected in your response to your current leaders. 3. Wait patiently for God to exalt you in his time and way. How would that look in your current context?

   _____

   _____

2. To whom do you want to make yourself accountable to put it into practice? Who would you like to pray with you on this?

   _____

   _____

Day 13

We work out daily what God has implanted in us –v.12-18.

Listen to the word – Picture this! You have been working out in your yard on a hot day! You have gotten sweaty and smelly! You can't even stand yourself! Yeah, I know, horrible image! Stay with me here! Your spouse says, "You are not touching me till you take a shower". So, you go take a nice, cleansing, refreshing shower and come back to your spouse. What is one of the first things he/she will probably do? He/she will smell you, drink in the freshness, and if you're lucky, you get a big hug or maybe even a passionate kiss. What made the difference? The shower did.

God's word has the capacity to cleanse, refresh, and transform our lives. This, however, is not automatic. Just as you do not get a shower by wishing it to be, you do not receive spiritual cleansing by wishing it to be either. We must have hearts that are ready to receive it. Now, go get your shower! Once you do, the world will "smell" the difference.

Read the word – The passage for today (2:12-18) needs to be seen in context. The first word of this passage is a linking word. It links what is about to be addressed to what was addressed. The word, "therefore", asks us to look back. What do we see in the previous passage? Jesus humbled himself and became obedient to the death on the cross. Therefore, you do this...With that in mind read on.

The Big Idea

_____

_____

_____

Thoughts, prayers, questions

_____

_____

_____

Meditation/memory verse:

_____

Read the brief commentary – What is going on in this passage? Start with the note under Read the word. Then start asking these questions. Are there any imperatives, any commands? These answer the question what? What does God expect of me in this case? So, start with them. The first is, "work out your own salvation..." How do I know that this is a command? It is elementary English grammar. "Work" is an active verb in this case. It is recorded in what is called an imperative tense. The subject doing the acting is "you". This personal pronoun, "you", is what is called the second person. (I or we is first. He, she, it, or they is third, and you is second). Therefore, Paul is speaking directly to the Philippians and in effect is saying to them, "You must work out your own salvation". This is a command. (I know most of us did not really appreciate grammar in school, but you cannot communicate well or understand what you are reading without it). Please stay with me.

Other questions to ask so that you can understand the passage are simple yet critical? We have answered one of the "what" questions. See if you can find another. Why, who, how, when, how much, are also very good questions to ask. For example, "why does God command us to work out our own salvation? How can we do that? Who is being addressed? Who is doing the speaking? I know this may sound and feel a little technical, but if you will learn to incorporate a little "investigative attitude" as you read, your time will become richer.

Read the passage again and respond.

1. What are the two commands given in this passage? (Clue – v. 12,14)

    _____

    _____

    _____

2. Why should we "work out our own salvation..."?

    _____

    _____

    _____

    _____

3. How can we "work out our own salvation..."? What does the word say? (v.14)

_____

_____

_____

_____

4. What will be the result of obeying these commands of God? (vs.15-18)?

_____

_____

_____

_____

Read the passage again and respond.

Principle #12 – Each day I will work out worshipfully, in practical living, what God has implanted graciously in me.

1. How will your word "shower" make a difference in your attitude toward your spouse today?_____your job and your boss? _____your employees?

   _____you fill in the blank with where you'd like to see change

   _____

   _____

2. Who will you share this with to keep you accountable and to be a support?

   _____

Notes:

Day 14

We model characteristics of humble servanthood v. -19-24

Listen to the word – Listen to the word today as you would listen to a friend you respect and care for very much.

Read the word – This passage (2:19-24) is one in which Paul demonstrates his aged wisdom in motivating and challenging believers. He has already offered himself as a model for the Philippians to follow. He magnified the need to humble obedience through the life of Christ. Now, he makes it very present and personal. My "son", Timothy, who has been with me, thinks just like me. As a matter of fact, his being there will be just like me being there. Read it as if Paul were speaking to your group in someone's home or Sunday school class.

The Big Idea

_____

_____

_____

Thoughts, prayers, questions

_____

_____

_____

Meditation/memory verse:

_____

Read the brief commentary – See Read the word above. Then, look back over the passage and your response in the big idea and such and write your own commentary as you would try to explain it to your group or Sunday school class.

_____

_____

_____

_____

_____

Read the passage again and respond

Principle #13 – I will seek to be a humble servant of Christ, like Timothy, mentored by a spiritual leader, compassionate, Christ-centered, and of proven character.

1. In what ways and in what contexts do you see yourself behaving as a humble servant?

    _____

    _____

2. Who will you seek to serve?

    _____

3. Do you have a spiritual mentor? Circle one. Yes/No? If so, who?
    If not, who would you like to ask to become your spiritual mentor?

What do you think you should look for in a spiritual mentor? (Hint: Maybe look at the model of Paul.) Make a working list not as a rigid checklist but more as a guide. Remember, there are no perfect people.

_____

_____

_____

_____

_____

Day 15

We model self- sacrifice for others in serving Christ –v. 25-30

Listen to the word – Listen beneath the words. Yes, words do mean something, but they are in fact symbols of our thoughts, our feelings, and our desires. Can you picture what is going on in this exchange? Imagine yourself in the company of Epaphroditus and Paul as they discuss the Philippians' concern for Epaphroditus.

Read the word – What mental videos ran through your mind as you imagined the situation with Paul and Epaphroditus in Philippians 2:25-30? Play it again before you record your thoughts.

The Big Idea (the central theme of this passage)

_____

_____

_____

Your thoughts, prayers, questions (what would be a good prayer you could pray for yourself based on Epaphroditus's example?)

_____

_____

Memorize/meditate:

Read the brief commentary – Pau had a special appreciation for Epaphroditus and the Philippians. Can you see why he makes so many warm comments concerning them? If he were here today you may hear him say to Epaphroditus, "I love you, man! And give him a bear hug. They were out on the front lines for the gospel. And let's not forget. Paul was in prison.

Read the passage again and respond.

1. What terms does Paul use in describing Epaphroditus (v. 25)?

    _____

    _____

2. Considering how Paul spoke of him, how would you describe his relationship with Epaphroditus?

    _____

    _____

3. What kind of relationship do you think the Philippians had with Epaphroditus based on how this story is described in v. 25-30?

    _____

    _____

    _____

4. If you had to describe how the relationship developed, what would it look like?

    _____

    _____

5. Is there an Epaphroditus in your life? Yes/No? Circle one. If so, who is it?_____Is there a group of Philippians in your life? Yes/No? If so, list as many as you can name here?

_____

_____

_____

6. Are you an Epaphroditus to someone? Yes/ No? If so, who?

_____

_____

If not, who could that be?

_____

_____

Read the passage again and respond

Principle #14 – I commit to give myself unselfishly for the needs of others and to continue growing in relationships.

1. Make a list of the specific ways in which you can seek to give unselfishly for the needs of others.

_____

_____

_____

_____

2. Prioritize the list based on what you feel the most passionate about

_____

_____

_____

3. Set target dates for when you would like to implement them

_____

_____

_____

4. For those of you who are more spontaneous, go out and start randomly finding someone to bless who would not expect it from you.

5. Who would you like to enlist as an ally in helping you accomplishing these things?

_____

_____

_____

Day 16 – Leg 2 - Summary of Transformation Principles

For this summary day and the for the following legs, we recommend that this be a time of extended worship utilizing your favorite worship songs and artists. Let loose and enjoy some time with God. Whether you prefer being loud and excitable or quiet and reflective or a little of both, let His Spirit lead you into it. Yes?

As you work through these principles in the form of evaluation questions allow God to reveal your heart. Reflect on these deeply and record honestly where you are. Celebrate the growth you have made. Acknowledge the areas for greater growth. Identify areas where you feel you need help from your spouse, your group, or your spiritual leader. Many intend on growing closer to Christ or to others but don't have a plan for doing so. Years later they are still intending on growing, but, have not.

You can grow in Christ beyond what you would ever think possible, but it doesn't happen on its own. We are not talking about self-made growth, but simply having a plan to use the means God has provided to grow in Christ in the context of Christian community. So, after this, you have listed the next 6 principles use the format provided or your own creation to develop your God-directed plan for growing in Christ in the areas you have identified.

Principle #9 - 2:1-4– Because of all that God has done for me and because of all the support he has placed around me I choose to be a humble team player and others focused

How am I doing at being a humble team player in all my spheres of influence (home, work, church, small group, recreation)? Am I relying on the encouraging resources God has placed around me? What needs to happen to walk more humbly as a team player?

_____

_____

_____

_____

Principle #10-2:5-8- My settled attitude toward God and for others will be humble obedience to God's will.

–Is my settled attitude toward God, like that of Jesus Christ, my master? Yes/ No? How am I doing at walking in humble obedience? Use your numbered scale to give yourself some kind of objective rating for how you are doing. 0 = My attitude sucks/I have a very long way to go.10 = I could be mistaken for the Pope, or a Jesus look alike. So, where are you?

_____

_____

Maybe a better question to ask would be how would my spouse, accountability partner, or small group answer it? Take some time to make an honest assessment of what you think they would say and record it here using the scale above

---

Principle #11-2:9-11- Like Christ, I will surrender promotion to the Father and look to him for his time and way.

Do I follow my Lord in not seeking to exalt or selfishly promote myself or am I caught up in fleshly oriented self-advancement? It is all about motive. How would you describe where you are now? Remember, it always helps more to be honest than self-deceived

---

Principle #12-2:12-18 - Each day I will work out worshipfully in practical living what God has implanted graciously in me.

Do I seek to live out each day in reverential awe and worship as I fulfill the purposes which God has implanted and empowered in me? Yes/No? How are you doing in your attempts to fulfill God's purposes?

What has God worked in you that you are struggling with working out in your life?

Who could you ask to become your ally?

_____

Principle #13-2:19-24 – I will seek to be a humble servant of Christ, like Timothy, mentored by a spiritual leader, compassionate, Christ-centered, and of proven character.

How is it going, becoming a mentored, Christ-centered, compassionate, humble servant? (Good is not the answer we are looking for. That would be too easy and not really helpful for you. Take some time to really examine your attitude, actions, and aspirations. Then record yourself evaluation here for yours and your family's benefit.

_____

_____

_____

_____

Maybe this scale would be helpful. On a scale of 1-10, 10 being perfection, how would you rate yourself in each category? Mentored_____; Christ-centered_____; compassionate_____ ; humble_____; and servant_____.

Principle #14-2:25-30 - I commit to give myself unselfishly for the needs of others and to continue growing in relationships.

How am I doing living unselfishly? How do I determine that? Try this. For the next week keep a record of what you do with your time? Try to think about why you do what you do? Record that for each segment of time you choose to quantify (Ex. 8-5 worked, 5-6 drove home; helped a coworker with a project, yelled at a guy who cut me off on the highway). Make sense?

_____

_____

_____

Who will you ask to join you? This is the kind of thing where it is most beneficial to be working through this journey in a group. Find someone (spouse, friend, accountability partner, and group) to share the plan and the results.

_____

_____

_____

_____

Notes:

My Action Plan for Pursuing Growth in Christ (Philippians 3: 13-14 - [13] Brothers, I do not consider that I have made it my own. But one thing I do: forgetting what lies behind and straining forward to what lays ahead, [14] I press on toward the goal for the prize of the upward call of God in Christ Jesus[2])

1. These are the areas of growth in my walk with Jesus. I praise him for them and I will celebrate these by

   _____

   _____

   _____

   _____

---

[2] *The Holy Bible: English Standard Version*. 2001 (Philippians 3:13–14). Wheaton: Standard Bible Society.

2. These are areas where I have seen some growth but want to see more growth. My plan for continued growth includes: SMART goals = Specific/ Measurable/Action oriented/Realistic/Time limited

_____

_____

_____

_____

3. These are areas where I feel like I am floundering and if I am truly honest with myself, I need help (we all do in areas of our lives so join the party). This is just a suggestion. Rather than pick a lot of areas why not focus on one for each category. Then, when you feel comfortable with your progress you can always add on to your growth list.

   a. I need help from my spouse/significant other in this area

   _____

   b. I need help from my group/close friends in this area

   _____

   c. I need help from my spiritual leader/elder/pastor/counselor in this area

   _____

   _____

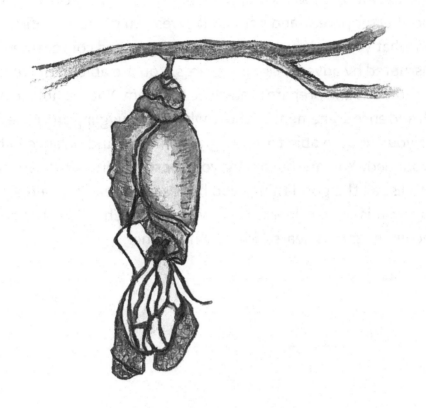

Leg 3

Becoming More Grounded in Christ

Day 17

In leg 3- Becoming More Grounded in Christ- Chapter 3-Partners in the gospel rely solely in the righteousness of Christ

We are well on our way in this journey of personal transformation. We have been encouraged, convicted, motivated, and challenged to move outside of our comfort zone. But is not that what transformation is all about? Change is unsettling. Change is disrupting. Change is at times confusing and uncomfortable. But, in the end, as you become moldable clay in the Master Potter's hands, the change produces greater intimacy with God, your spouse, and those close. It enables you to be a much better parent and person. It gives you greater confidence in who you are and what you do. You walk in greater peace and contentment. Your joy is not as disrupted by adverse circumstances. You are able to better anticipate Satan's temptations and prepare in advance for them. You are able to be a source of strength and encouragement to those who are struggling and have not grown as much as you. You are able to show grace, mercy, and balance in helping to heal the wounded. You are becoming your best self in Christ. So, take a few moments to list all the good things you have seen already, as a result of being on this journey. It is ok to celebrate your victories in Christ. He has enabled you and it is encouraging to rehearse what he has done.

_____

_____

_____

_____

_____

We rely solely in the righteousness of Christ – 3:1-6

Listen to the word –Listen for nuggets. Sometimes we slip into this mode of functional operation. We hear the words, but we really do not hear the meaning. It is like we have zoned out and have been transported to some other place. Then when we come back we ask ourselves the question, what did I just read? Try this. Before listening to the word, get quiet. Close your eyes and use that vivid imagination of yours. See yourself in a synagogue in the days of Jesus (work with me here). You are standing in the first row. Jesus goes to the front and opens the scroll to read his Father's words. He begins, "Finally, my brothers/sisters!"

Read the word – Today, the passage has some unusual concepts in it. Do not get hung up on what is not familiar.

The Big Idea

_____

_____

_____

Thoughts, prayers, questions

_____

_____

_____

Meditation/memory verse:

_____

Read the brief commentary –This section could be outlined the following way.

1. His righteousness is my source of joy – v.1.
2. His righteousness is my safeguard against dilution (weakening) of soul – v.2.
3. His righteousness is the indelible (unbreakable) seal on my heart –v.3-6.

The first verse includes another one of Paul's imperatives to rejoice in the Lord. What follows is a warning against those who would have us derive (draw) our confidence from things that praise our fleshly accomplishments. Then, he points us to our true source of confidence, Christ, and his righteousness.

Read the passage again and respond.

1. What is the significance of Paul beginning this chapter by reminding the Philippians to rejoice in the Lord? Consider the larger context –chapters and Paul's situation

_____

_____

_____

2. Describe a time in your life when the circumstances were not conducive (favorable) to "rejoicing in the Lord". How did you respond/react? What was underneath that reaction? As you have become more aware of God's purpose and presence through this transformation journey in what way would you envision yourself responding to similar circumstances now?

_____

_____

_____

3. In Paul's warning to the Philippians, against what was he warning them (see verses 2-6)?

_____

4. What would you consider a modern-day problem that is analogous (similar) to their problem? Describe it and how you would respond as a result of your transformation journey?

_____

_____

_____

_____

Read the passage again and respond.

Principle #15 I will rest in the righteousness of Christ as my source of joy, protection against dilution, and the seal on my heart.

1. Since resting in Christ's righteousness, is an internal thing, how will you know when you are?

_____

_____

_____

2. Maybe this will help. Ask yourself three questions: a. What am I looking to as the source of my joy? As you self-evaluate, be honest. It will not help if you are not

_____

_____

b. Am I feeling watered down in my soul? Am I feeling hollow, lifeless, and empty? If so, where is my mind most of the time? Where are my emotions most of the time? Where is my energy being spent?

_____

_____

_____

c. Respond to these questions based on the text. What or whose am I? Whose or what seal is on my heart now? Under whose or what banner am I operating? To whom or to what do I "belong"?

_____

_____

_____

_____

Day 18

We value gaining Christ over everything –3:7-8.

Listen to the word –As you are listening to the word today, do not just listen to the words. Listening to them is a very important part of hearing from God. But, seek to develop your "inner ear", hearing the Spirit with the core of your being. Let his life speak to your life. Ask him to search your heart and let you know yourself and him more intimately. Then as you listen, you will be amazed at what God can show you. Record those messages below.

Read the passage – v. 7-8

The Big Idea

_____

_____

_____

Thoughts, prayers, questions

_____

_____

_____

Memorize and Meditate:

_____

Read the brief commentary - Paul was no monk in a monastery sealed off from the outside world. When he talks about gain he had before Christ, it was significant. He was not only a Hebrew of Hebrews. He had been trained at the feet of Gamaliel, a nationally renowned rabbi, and more than likely would have followed in his shoes as Israel's top rabbi. He would have had national recognition, respect, honor, and financial support. Paul would have been a well-known and respected household name. He knew personally what loss for Christ was.

Read the passage again and respond

1. What "gains", valuables, whether material, physical, relational, or psychological did you or do you have? Some suggestions: Material wealth – 6 figure income, Lexus, $800,000 home? A body like a model or a UFC fighter(less the cauliflower ear)? Friends all over the US? A career with power and respect in your organization or the corporate world? Maybe you are a well-known respected pastor or a mom who has raised 5 children who are successful in their vocations? Make your own list

    _____

    _____

    _____

2. What is it that you would feel like you were "going to die" if you lost?

_____

On a scale of 1-10, where do you see yourself? If you were to lose any or all of your "valuables", where would you be? 1= would be utterly devastated and unable to recuperate any time in the near future. 10 =would be able to fully grieve the loss, be grateful for the time they were with me, and able to surrender them over to God. 12345678910? Circle one. Why did you choose that number? What would it take to move closer to 10

_____

_____

_____

3. What have you gained in coming to Christ? This is intentionally a generalized question so that you will take time to reflect seriously on all that you have gained in coming to Christ. Take as much time as you need in terms of minutes, hours, days...Then record in detail what you have realized. You will probably need another sheet, or two, or more.

_____

_____

_____

_____

_____

Read the passage again and respond.

Principle #16 – I value gaining Christ whatever it may cost. In every situation, context, and relationship it will be Christ first.

Use your time in what would have been application questions to process #2 above.

Day 19

> We release the pursuit of self-righteousness for God's gift of righteousness – 3:9

Listen to the word – We each, like Samuel, call out to God, "Speak Lord for your servant hears".

Read the word – v. 9 – Do not miss the power and significance of this short passage by assuming that its simplicity means it is shallow. God has a way of saying a great deal with few words.

The Big Idea – Put this in your own words

_____

_____

_____

Thoughts, questions, and prayers:

_____

_____

Read the passage and the brief commentary and respond v. 9 – Paul differentiates God's righteousness from self-righteousness in this passage. This is a significant distinction for practical living. Self-righteousness is derived from adherence to the law. In the book of Deuteronomy the word teaches that he who would depend on his own righteousness to gain and maintain a right standing with God must do so by keeping the law. James states very clearly that if you keep all the commandments and yet offend in one you are guilty of breaking all (James 2:10-12). The law is a comprehensive system that is applied as a single unit. You, either keep the whole law or you do not, no gray area in between. Though we know this in theory, many of us still attempt to earn God's favor daily by keeping the law, or by doing the "Christian thing".

The other righteousness, which Paul describes, is one that comes by faith from God. In theological terms, it is an imputed righteousness. God credits Christ's righteousness to our account and counts it as our own. This includes righteousness that initially puts us in right relationship with God and that maintains a right relationship with God. Righteousness by law is performance based. Righteousness by faith is grace based. What's in your account?

1. As you think about how you operate in your relationship with God, under which type of righteousness would you say you are functioning in actuality?

    _____

    _____

    Describe how this looks in practice

    _____

    _____

    _____

    For example: How do you handle it when you sin? Do you mentally or emotionally beat up on yourself till you feel like it is sufficient? Or do you go to God, confess it, accept, and thank him for his forgiveness, and then step out by faith to live another day better?

    _____

2. Describe how it would look for you to walk in Christ's righteousness.

    _____

    _____

    _____

    What would be different in your thought life? Your emotional responses? Choices? Behaviors? Interactions in your relationships? (This one requires you to envision yourself in those contexts and respond based upon your understanding of living a grace-based life relying on the righteousness of Christ rather than trying to perform to gain or maintain God's acceptance)

_____

_____

_____

_____

Read the passage again and respond.

Principle #17 I release the pursuit of merit (earning) based righteousness in exchange for reliance on the righteousness of Christ.

1. With a better understanding of merit/performance based self-righteous living, make a list of the ways you can see yourself releasing that?

   _____

   _____

   _____

2. Now create a list of how you would see you yourself living differently in contrast to each one.

   _____

   _____

   _____

3. With whom would you feel the most comfortable to share this and ask for support?

   _____

4. Since this will be an ongoing challenge, it might be a good idea to share regularly with your group.

Day 20

We make it our passion to know Christ experientially 3:10-11.

Listen to the word –Part of listening involves seeing. Picture yourself with Christ (as a "fly on his shoulder") as he walked on the earth, went to the cross, and rose from the dead (See 2:8).

Read the word –Read Philippians 3:10-11.

The Big Idea

_____

_____

Thoughts, questions, and prayers – What questions would you like answered from this section?

_____

_____

_____

Verse for meditation and memorization

_____

_____

Read the brief commentary – Philippians 3:10-11 is connected to the previous verses in that this is the purpose for which one has been given God's righteousness. You are enabled to enter an experiential relationship with Christ, knowing him in ever increasing degrees and being transformed by his death for sins and his resurrection power. It is through his death that we die to our sins and through his resurrection power that we are continually made alive in him. He awakens and enables the fruit of the Spirit to be a genuine daily reality. Truly, it is only by surrendering to this process (dying to sin's power and being made alive daily in Christ) that we can live the life to which he has called us.

Read the passage again and respond.

1. Describe the ways/avenues in which you know your spouse, significant other, or close friend. How were you introduced? How did you grow in your acquaintance? How did you move from merely being an acquaintance to being a friend? To being close? To being emotionally intimate?

    _____

    _____

    _____

    _____

2. How would you describe the progression of your relationship with Christ in these terms

    _____

    _____

    _____

    _____

3. Is this relationship where you want it to be? If so, how could it be even better? If not, how would you like it to be different? Describe the ways for each one.

    _____

    _____

    _____

    _____

4. Sometimes there are internal "roadblocks" or "barriers" to growth in relationships (Ex. Keeping a secret that hinders trust, not speaking up for a practice that hurts you, nagging baggage from the past...). What may be some of those in your relationship with Christ?

_____

_____

_____

_____

5. Who would you like to enlist to assist you with this? Who do you trust? Share this with them and if you feel safe, with the group for support.

_____

_____

_____

_____

Read the passage again and respond.

Principle #18 – I make it my passion to know Christ experientially, in his suffering, death, and resurrection.

1. Think and pray over this. Discuss it with your spouse, significant other, or group. Write out a general plan for how you envision getting to know Christ in an increasing manner. It does not have to be complicated although if you are that kind of personality, that is fine. It just needs to be clear enough to implement.

    _____

    _____

    _____

    _____

    To whom would you like to make yourself accountable for implementing this personal growth in Christ plan? _____

    When do you plan to talk with them about it? _____

Day 21

> We make pursuing Christ a lifelong occupation rather than a short-term project- v. 12-16

Listen to the word Part of listening well to someone involves hearing the tone and pursuing the underlying meaning of what their words represent. As you listen to the word today, try to listen for tone (emotion, mood, etc.) and underlying significance.

Read the word – Read Philippians 3:12-16. As you read the passage today, remember that the Bible is God's love letter to his highly treasured covenant people. It is his love letter to you, the one he gave his life to redeem and transform.

The Big Idea (Try writing this in language your kids could understand)

_____

_____

_____

Thoughts, questions, and prayers (Sometimes God has specific words of encouragement, direction, conviction as you read his word and listen to the Spirit. Write those down here for further consideration and feedback from your spouse, friend, or group)

_____

_____

_____

_____

Meditation/memory verses:

_____

Read the brief commentary Philippians 3:12-16. These verses reflect Paul's "winning attitude" game plan. In short, it is this. Claim him who has claimed you. Don't linger in past victories or failures. Pursue the goal of God's upward call. Hold on to what you have. This is just a very short practical comment on the passage. These comments will continue to remain short, to encourage you to discover for yourself, by the Spirit, God's "hidden treasure" for your soul.

Read the passage again and respond.

1. What is the motivating source, according to Paul, for his pursuit of Christ? V.12

    _____

    _____

2. How would you rate Paul's passion for pursuing Christ, as he relates it in this passage? On a scale of 1-10, 1 being minimal, 10 being off the chart.

    _____? How would you rate yourself? _____. Where do you desire to be? _____.

3. If you were to use the short "winning attitude" game plan above as guidelines for growing in your passionate pursuit of Christ, where would you want to focus your attention? (read v. 12-16 as many times as needed to feel confident you grasp the significance of the passage).

    a. Do I actively claim him as my own in every sphere of my life? _Yes/No_ ? If so, to what degree? How often?

        _____

        _____

    b. Do I linger in past victories or failures or do I learn from them and move forward? _____. To what degree do I need to let go or process through the past? And in what areas? Take time to really think and pray about this. It does not help to continue to live alone with unresolved areas. They keep coming up.

        _____

_____

_____

c. How are you doing at pursuing God's upward call toward becoming Christ-like? For this one ask someone who has a "proven record" of being objective. They will tell you what they really think and see. After prayer, reflection, and consultation with your objective person record your results.

_____

_____

_____

_____

d. How well are you doing at holding on to where you are and not slipping back in your spiritual progress? We all have somewhat of a "three steps forward, two steps back" movement generally. But how do you see yourself? Circle whatever is appropriate.

    i.   Very inconsistent- unsatisfied
    ii. Beginning to become consistent- not really satisfied but getting there
    iii. Growing in consistency, but still struggling regularly
    iv. Walking consistently, slipping occasionally
    v.   Steady and consistent- I am very content in my walk with the Lord and hunger for more.

Read the passage again and respond.

Principle # 19 – I will pursue with persistence, humility, and passion growth in Christlikeness.

1. The questions above have been provided to assist you in implementing a practical plan for growing in Christlikeness. It is just a plan. Have you or will you set it in motion? Do you have your own plan to set in motion? The main consideration here is to have some sort of plan. The axiom

(principle), however trite (simple), is still true. Fail to plan, plan to fail. Respond here

_____

_____

_____

_____

2. Share your plan with those you trust and would like to enlist to assist you in your progress. (A personally beneficial study, if you are curious as to how the believers' community functioned in the early days of the church, would be to look up the phrase "one another" in the New Testament and see what kinds of activities are associated with them. You can do this by using a concordance, either hard copy, Bible software program, or online. Some Bibles have a concise concordance but would not have an exhaustive list of all the passages. Hint: There is also a One Another Passage list in the appendix). I plan on sharing my plan with

_____

_____

_____

_____

Notes:

Day 22

We watch for those who would dilute the truth – 3:17-21

Listen to the word – As you listen today, imagine yourself to be a crime investigator. Look for clues that would reveal things that dilute the truth of God working in your life.

Read the word – Read Philippians 3:17-21. As you read this passage, try to put yourself in Paul's shoes. He was instrumental in helping the Philippians grow in their faith. He saw threats to that development around them and warned them of those threats. How would you respond to someone trying to get your family member into a cult?

The Big Idea

_____

_____

Thoughts, questions, and prayers (How could you pray for your family's and friends' protection against having their spiritual life diluted [weakened])?

_____

_____

_____

Memory verse/meditation

_____

Read the brief commentary – In this passage Paul provides an affirmative path to follow and warns against those who would hinder your walk with Christ. Verses 18-19 is a strong warning against following the people, whose motives reflect enmity against the cross of Christ, pursue selfish ends, and ultimately worship themselves rather than God. Finally, verses 20-21 calls us to watch and wait for the Savior who will complete the transformation he began in us when we first trusted him.

Read the passage again and respond

1. Describe Paul's "example". Verses 7-16 reveal a great deal about Paul's lifestyle. What, in his life, is worthy of emulating(following)?

   _____

   _____

   _____

   _____

2. Describe the characteristics of those he considers "enemies of the cross".

   _____

   _____

   _____

   _____

3. The word "For" in verse 20 ties these final two verses to v. 17-19. According to these verses, why would we want to follow Paul's example and avoid the model of "enemies of the cross"?

   _____

   _____

   _____

   _____

   Read the passage again and respond.

Principle #20 – I will follow my models, beware of those who dilute my walk, and wait expectantly for transformation from Christ.

1. Who is there in your life or someone you would like to follow as an example of a Christ-follower?

   _____

How might you "link up" with them to see if they would be open to invest in your life?

_____

2. Who are people you feel do have or would have a negative influence in your life?

_____

How will you respond to them?

_____

_____

3. What are you looking forward to most as you anticipate Christ's return?

_____

_____

_____

4. How will that keep you on track with Christ?

_____

_____

_____

Notes:

Day 23 – Leg 3 – Summary of Transformation Principles

For this summary day and the for the following legs, we recommend that this be a time of extended worship utilizing your favorite worship songs and artists. Let loose and enjoy some time with God. Whether you prefer being loud and excitable or quiet and reflective or a little of both, let His Spirit lead you into it. Yes?

As you work through these principles in the form of evaluation questions allow God to expose your heart. Reflect on these deeply and record honestly where you are. Celebrate the growth you have made. Acknowledge the areas for greater growth needed. Identify areas where you feel you need help from your spouse, your group, or your spiritual leader. Many intend on growing closer to Christ or to others but don't have a plan for doing so. Years later they are still intending on growing, but haven't.

You can grow in Christ beyond what you would ever think possible, but it doesn't happen on its own. We are not advocating self-made growth, but simply having a plan to use the means God has provided to grow in Christ in the context of Christian community. Therefore, after this, you have listed the next 6 principles. Use the format provided or your own creation to develop your God-directed plan for growing in Christ in the areas you have identified.

Principle # 15 – 3:1-6 - I will rest in the righteousness of Christ as my source of joy, protection against dilution, and the seal on my heart.

On a scale of 1-10, from lowest to highest, where would you put the average of your focus on Christ vs. self for the source of your joy, protection against dilution, and what rules your heart? Circle one – 1-2-3-4-5-6-7-8-9-10.

What would it take to move up the scale?

_____

_____

Who might be your best ally to help you with this?

_____

Principle #16 –3:7-8 - I value gaining Christ above all, whatever it may cost, in every situation, context, and relationship.

What losses have you experienced, either from following Christ or just your life circumstances?

_____

_____

_____

Have you mourned them fully? Circle one- Yes /No/ Not Sure. It is important to mourn our losses fully so that we are not "stuck" in the past. (We do not forget the past, but we grow from it and take the lessons with us. If there are areas that you have not mourned fully I would encourage you to record them here, pour out your heart in honest brokenness to God, share with your spouse or group whomever you feel is appropriate. If necessary, contact your pastor or qualified grief counselor).Below are my losses:

_____

_____

_____

This is my plan for dealing with them:

_____

_____

_____

Principle #17 –3:9 -I release the pursuit of merit-based righteousness in exchange for reliance on the righteousness of Christ.

Am I holding on to my own efforts to please God? Treating others as I would want to be treated, doing "good" to all, etc? Or am I resting in his finished work on the cross for my forgiveness and right standing with God, and then doing all those good things out of a grateful heart? This is a soul-searching question. You probably know what the "right" answer should be. But that is not the question here. You have trusted Christ as your savior. That is settled. But, in your day-to-day living, are you resting on His merit or yours? Record your thoughts here. Grace generated living is significantly different that guilt generated living

_____

Principle #18 – 3:10-11 - I make it my passion to know Christ experientially, his suffering, death, and resurrection.

How would you rate your passion level to know Christ experientially on a scale of 0-10, with 10 being the highest? Circle one- 0-1-2-3-4-5-6-7-8-9-10.

How would you rate your satisfaction level for where you are on that scale? Circle one- Totally satisfied-Satisfied-Unsure-Not Satisfied-Dissatisfied-Very Dissatisfied.

From what you have discovered to this point in the journey of transformation, what would you incorporate in your plan to move from where you are to where you want to be?

_____

_____

_____

Principle #19 – 3:12-16 - I will pursue with persistence, humility, and passion, growth in Christlikeness.

What has been your plan for growing in Christlikeness? Describe it in terms as concrete and specific as possible

_____

_____

_____

How is it working for you?

_____

Here are a few things to reflect on and record. God sees us as perfect in Christ (v.12). Am I striving to live out what God already considers me to be? Or, am I running on Christian autopilot- I'm a believer, I go to church, I do Christian things, blah, blah, blah...? Respond.

_____

_____

_____

Am I stuck in the past (victories or failures), or have I learned from it and continue to grow?

_____

Am I like a track runner in pursuing the goal of God's call on my life? Or have I come to accept status quo?

_____

Am I grasping the extent to which I have grown and long for more, or have I become spiritually lethargic and undisciplined?

_____

Principle #20 - 3:17-21 - I will follow my models, beware of those who dilute my walk, and wait expectantly for transformation from Christ.

Do I have positive, godly role models in my life or am I looking up to those who have a more negative impact on me? Who is influencing whom?

_____

_____

Am I on solid ground in my Christian worldview to be able to recognize subtle unhealthy influences? Yes/No Circle one. If not, what might you think would be helpful to get to that place?

_____

_____

Am I waiting with anticipation for Christ's return or would I rather he did not come back soon because I am not ready, or I want to complete my agenda?

My Action Plan for Pursuing Growth in Christ (Philippians 3: 13-14 - [13] Brothers, I do not consider that I have made it my own. But one thing I do: forgetting what lies behind and straining forward to what lays ahead, [14] I press on toward the goal for the prize of the upward call of God in Christ Jesus[3])

1. These are the areas of growth in my walk with Jesus. I praise him for them and I will celebrate these by

   _____

   _____

2. These are areas where I have seen some growth but want to see more growth. My plan for continued growth includes: SMART goals = Specific/ Measurable/Action oriented/Realistic/Time limited

   _____

   _____

   _____

   _____

3. These are areas where I feel like I am floundering and if I am truly honest with myself, I need help (we all do in areas of our lives so join the party). This is just a suggestion. Rather than pick a lot of areas why not focus on one for each category. Then, when you feel comfortable with your progress you can always add on to your growth list.

   a. I need help from my spouse/significant other in this area

   _____

---

[3] *The Holy Bible: English Standard Version.* 2001 (Philippians 3:13–14). Wheaton: Standard Bible Society.

b. I need help from my group/close friends in this area

_____

_____

c. I need help from my spiritual leader/elder/pastor/counselor in this area

_____

_____

Leg 4

Becoming More Wholly Connected with Others, Self, and God

Day 24

In leg 4- Becoming More Wholly Connected with Others, Self, and God-Chapter 4-Partners in the gospel build a unified team that stands

This is now the fourth and final leg of this journey of transformation. There will be other journeys. As we allow God's Spirit through his word to focus our attention on Christ in the context of a passionate surrendered community, we will see God transform us into the image and character of his son. That is his plan for us (see Romans 8:28-29).

In our journey so far, we have persevered through adversity learning that Christ is always the object of our gaze. We have begun to learn that serving is God's highest call, that true fellowship is passionate action, and that through persistent believing prayer we grow in the practical expression of God's love. In short, we are learning to live worthy of the gospel.

We have kneeled in awe of the humility, suffering, and glorious victory of Christ. He entered our world and identified with us on every level, though without sin, so that we could walk like him and ultimately be transformed into his bodily design. We have begun to learn humble serving through observing Paul, Timothy, and Epaphroditus.

We have begun to properly value the finished work of Christ, by relying and resting in his righteousness for daily progress. We have begun to realize more poignantly (emphatically) that following Christ is a daily hot pursuit rather than a one-time event. We have begun to learn from the past defeats and victories rather than becoming stuck in the past. We have begun to learn that he is more than enough to keep us from becoming diluted in our souls.

Now, let us pick up our gear, strap it on, and continue our journey. Are you ready?

We build a unified team that stands- 4:1-3

Listen to the word – As you listen to the word today see how many emotion words you can identify. Note them in your "thoughts, questions, and prayers section". What do you think is the significance of the particular emotional words that are used?

Read the word –Read Philippians 4:1-3 and try to visualize the encounter that Paul encouraged to occur.

The Big Idea

_____

_____

Thoughts, prayers, questions

_____

_____

_____

Memory verse/meditation: What truth would you like to carry with you throughout the day? You might want to enter it in as your device wallpaper, write it on a 3x5 card, put it on your refrigerator, mirror, or dash board (please, don't wreck because you were reading it at the wrong time).

_____

_____

Read the passage, read the brief commentary: Here are questions to use to develop your commentary. To what does the first word in the first verse point? (Hint: look back at the previous chapter)

_____

_____

What is the significance of this

_____

_____

What is the imperative (command) in this sentence?

_____

What is its significance? Why is it important

_____

_____

What terms does Paul use to refer to the Philippians?

_____

_____

How does this perspective affect the mannerhe addresses the issue with the two women?

_____

_____

What is Paul's counsel for the women?_____The true companion?

_____

Paul saw their fractured relationship as too vital in the partnership of the gospel to leave it dangling without resolution.

God calls us, as much as is humanly possible, to resolve those relational loose ends in our lives. Otherwise, though we try to hide it or deny it, we are diluted in our walk with God and others. We cannot violate His established relational "laws" and not reap the consequences. We may be able to go on living our lives, but the unresolved relational issues continue, like a little mouse gnawing on the inside of the wall, to wear away our internal health. Eventually, the mouse will get through and wreak havoc on our "house". He will get into our food (feeding on Christ). He will defecate (leave droppings) on our floors (create emotional, relational, and spiritual messes). He will infect us with whatever diseases he may carry (bitterness, malice, jealousy, envy, lust, hate...).

Read the passage the third time and respond.

Principle #21 – I will pursue unity in Christ by seeking to resolve my relational conflicts and trust Christ with the unresolvable.

1. Read and respond honestly. This will help you consciously know where you are.

a. As I pray and reflect on my relationships, I am...at peace knowing that all is well or I have done all that I can to resolve conflicts _____.

b. I know that there is/are a relationship /relationships I need to resolve and I am committed to doing that as soon as is feasible _____.

c. I know that there are issues I have not resolved but I am not emotionally ready to do so, and I feel stuck. I need help to move forward _____.

d. I am still hurt and bitter over what was done to me and I am not ready to deal with it _____.

e. Just to think about it makes me *@%$*&!!!!!!!!!! _____.

2. If you feel comfortable enough to talk with a safe person about this, who would that person be?_____. Sometimes we all need help outside of our family and friends. Do you know someone (pastor, counselor, therapist...) who you would want to see?

_____

_____

Day 25

We live a lifestyle of joy v. 4

Listen to the word – Sometimes when we have heard something repeatedly we tend to "shut down" our listening mode and stray mentally. Be aware of that possibility and intentionally focus on hearing all God may want to speak out of his word.

Read the word – Read verses 1-9 to get the immediate context. Try reading a different translation. Sometimes a different translation provides a nuance to the meaning and provides a new insight.

The Big Idea

_____

_____

Thoughts, prayers, questions

_____

_____

Memory verse

_____

Read brief commentary –Today we are going to do a brief word study in the book of Philippians. When a Biblical writer uses the same word or words from its root repeatedly, there may be a significant message God is seeking to communicate. to see this more fully, we search for all the instances in the book. The words in this case are joy, rejoice, etc. Find the passages, briefly check out the immediate context (the surrounding verses), and record what seems to be significant (Philippians 1:18;2:28; 3:1; 4:4,10;1:4,25;2:2,29;4:1). (Just for your information and edification – there are 299 references to joy or derivatives in the Old Testament and 134 references to joy in the New Testament. That is a total of 499 references. Do you think God desires for us to know his joy? This does not include similarity in concept (for example –dancing, singing, exulting, etc.). What did you discover?

_____

_____

_____

_____

_____

Read the passage again and respond.

1. What is the command/imperative in this passage?

   _____

2. What does the word mean and what is its significance?

   _____

_____

_____

3. Does it seem odd to you that this seems to be a command to feel a certain way?_____ Does it seem counterintuitive? _____ How do you explain this since it is clearly a command. God does not give us commands he has not equipped to obey?

_____

_____

4. How does your word study on joy throughout the rest of Philippians affect your understanding of this passage?

_____

_____

_____

Read the passage again and respond.

Principle #22- I choose today to rejoice in the people, circumstances, gifts, and opportunities given by God.

1. How would you personally apply this in your life context?

_____

_____

_____

2. What would you see as potential obstacles to incorporating this in your lifestyle?

_____

_____

3. What are some of the "assets" you have available to apply this in your lifestyle?

_____

_____

_____

4. With whom would you like to share this and to what extent would you elicit (ask for) their support and encouragement?

_____

_____

_____

Notes:

Day 26

We live a meek lifestyle – 4:5

Listen to the word – Ask this as you listen. What am I hearing God say about himself through the word that enables me to know him more intimately?

Read the word – Read verses 1-7 to get the immediate context.

The Big Idea

_____

_____

Thoughts, prayers, questions

Read the brief commentary – Here, again, we have a short passage. To get a fuller understanding of its significance we want to do a brief expanded word study. This would include its use in the book of Philippians and, in our case, in the other books of the New Testament. This word is used seldom, once here, and in four other places in the New Testament. Look up these references to see how the same Greek word is used in other passages. In this way you get a fuller, richer picture of its significance is in this passage (1 Timothy 3:3; Titus 3:2; James 3:17; 1 Peter 2:18). You can also read this passage in other versions. After doing this, record your findings and record your understanding of its significance.

_____

_____

_____

_____

Read the passage again and respond.

1. According to your previous search, how would you write the first part of verse 5 in your own words?

_____

_____

2. Given the context of the previous passage (verses 2-3) and a number of Paul's statements in other parts of Philippians (1:27-28; 2:1-4; 3:15-16) what was the significance of this directive for the Philippians?

_____

_____

_____

_____

What added significance does the second part of this verse have on what you have already discovered?

_____

_____

_____

_____

Read the passage again and respond.

Principle #23 –I am called to maintain a gentle disposition in all of my interactions.

1. Describe how it would look for your "reasonableness to be known to all".

    _____

    _____

2. In your current interactions how would you rate yourself on a scale of 1-10, 1 being argumentative and critical, 10 being reasonable, gentle in every way, almost mistaken as Christ? Write the rating you give yourself after each of the following areas of relationship.

    a. Family member's _____?
    b. Work environment _____?
    c. Church small group _____?
    d. People you "hang out" with on a periodic basis _____?
    e. Casual acquaintances _____?

3. As you look at how you have rated yourself in the various spheres of influence does anything stand out? If so, what is its significance?

    _____

    _____

4. What practical steps does this new perspective move you to take if any?

    _____

_____

_____

_____

5. Take some time to share your findings with your spouse or group.

Notes:

Day 27

We pray believing – v. 6-7

Listen to the word – What am I learning concerning effective prayer as I listen today? Listen for implicit (not so obvious) truths about prayer as well as the explicit (obvious) ones (examples, relationship expression, etc...)

Read the word –Read Philippians 4:6-7 in a few different versions.

The Big Idea - What is the central idea of this passage? Try to state it in one concise pregnant statement

_____

Thoughts, prayers, questions

_____

_____

_____

Memory verse/meditation

_____

Read the brief commentary- These two verses are pregnant with instruction on prayer. It is critical to remember the larger historical context, i.e. Paul wrote this from prison. He was not in a high ivory tower, safe and secure from the "down and dirty" battles of the real world. He knew what it was like to go through pain and suffering. "Through" is the operative word in the previous sentence. Much of the time we want to be delivered "from" the times of trial not "through". Having been on this journey for 39 years, I can tell you that most of the time, for me, it has been "through" the pain and suffering. As you read these verses on prayer, note what is "oddly" left out.

Read the passage again and respond.

1. What might be considered the first step in practicing effective prayer? (Hint: See verse 6a – The Greek indicates being anxious was already a reality. It could be translated, "Stop being anxious!")

   _____

   _____

2. According to this verse what are four components of "effective" prayer (v. 6)?

   _____

   _____

   _____

3. What is the promise or result that Paul indicates will come out of pursuing God in this manner?

   _____

   _____

4. What do these other passages written by the same divinely inspired human writer add to your understanding of the nature and practice of effective prayer? (1 Corinthians 14:15; Romans 12:12; Ephesians 6:18; Colossians 4:2; 1 Thessalonians 3:10, 5:17; 1 Timothy 2:8, 5:5; Romans 8:15,26; Galatians 4:6; Ephesians 3:14ff).

_____
_____
_____
_____

Read the passage again and respond.

Principle # 24 – I will give my anxious thoughts over to God in prayer and anticipate receiving his peace.

1. It is time for a "what if..." question. If you were on your dying bed and you wanted to give your last best "advice" to your children on how to pray effectively, using only what you have just encountered, what would that counsel be? Take the time to personalize it in a short letter format to one of your children.

    _____
    _____
    _____
    _____

2. If our relationship with God is the most important relationship, and if our family members are the most important humans in our lives, then would we not be well advised to help link the two? Pray about this. If it would be feasible, why not consider doing what you just did as a "what if"? Think it through with your spouse. Maybe talk with your group. Then record whatever you believe God would have you do here.

    _____
    _____
    _____
    _____

Day 28

We meditate on things that are virtuous v. 8-9

Listen to the word – Where would you like to focus?

Read the word – Read Philippians 4:8-9

The Big Idea

_____

_____

Thoughts, prayers, questions – What are the first thoughts which come to mind when you read this passage?

_____

_____

Memory verse/meditation

_____

Read the brief commentary – Paul gives a summary statement. "Finally," clues us in on some of the most pertinent material. Many of our issues can be resolved, corrected, processed, and redeemed through having our thinking arrested and transformed. What is on your mind today? Someone once made the statement that, "You are what you are by the people you know and the books you read." Since each of these influences what we think, might it not be a good idea to be wise in whom we know and what we read?

Read the passage again and respond

1. What are the two imperatives in this passage?

_____

_____

2. What significance does this have for your current lifestyle?

_____

_____

3. What role and value does Paul attribute to his example?

_____

_____

4. Recommendation (v.8) – In order to get a clear picture of what each of these foci for our meditation and sustained thought are, look them up in a Strong's concordance, Bible Dictionary, Bible Commentary, or online resource. What did you come up with? I'll start out – whatever things are true- real, honest, of integrity...

_____

noble

_____

just

_____

pure

_____

lovely

_____

good report

_____

virtuous

_____

praiseworthy

_____

Read the passage again and respond.

Principle #25 –I choose to meditate on Christ-like virtues and put into practice what I have observed from godly role models.

1. How could you apply this and make it a part of your lifestyle? (Example: I am working on developing an ethical decision-making model that includes these virtues and others for my therapy practice). How about you? This could include any arena home, work, new business start-up, church, school, etc.

   _____

   _____

   _____

   _____

2. With whom would you like to share your plan as an ally and for accountability?

   _____

3. When do you anticipate implementing this plan?

   _____

   I purpose to begin implementing this plan by (date) _____and I would like to have (name(s)) _____as my ally.

Notes:

Day 29

We care for one another deeply –v. 10-13

Listen to the word – As you listen today, listen for cues to God's provision (material, spiritual, emotional, relational, etc.). In the thoughts, prayers, and questions section jot down some of those "cues" you heard.

Read the word – Read Philippians 4:10-13.

he Big Idea

_____

_____

_____

Thoughts, prayers, questions

_____

_____

_____

_____

Memorize/meditation

_____

Read the brief commentary – In this passage Paul affirms the Philippians for their ongoing investment and responsiveness to his needs. He also relays to them a very important truth related to personal needs and the source of their supply. This is the context for an oft quoted verse.

Read the passage again and respond.

1. What was the specific nature of what Paul affirmed in the Philippians?

_____

_____

2. What is the essential truth Paul shared with the Philippians with regards to personal needs?

_____

_____

_____

3. What word best describes the virtue that Paul is highlighting?

_____

4. How would you define it for your personal context?

_____

_____

_____

_____

5. What do you think is at the heart of the opposite of this virtue?

_____

_____

_____

_____

Read the passage again and respond.

Principle #26 – I choose to walk in contentment trusting Christ to provide what he knows I need in each, and every situation.

1. Make a list of what you consider your needs to be. This can cover short term, long term, whatever you want to list. Recommendation: Try to be comprehensive.

_____

_____

_____

_____

_____

2. Now, prioritize them by putting a number beside each one starting at 1 for the most important, 2 for the next, etc.

3. For each one, try to determine how you would rate your contentment based on how they have been met or addressed in your life. Use a scale to do this. Rate your contentment from 1 to 10, 10 being completely content and 1 being completely discontent. If it helps, make a new list with each need represented by one word, and then place the appropriate contentment number beside it.

_____

_____

_____

_____

4. Contentment works on a continuum. No one or at least very few people operate at a 10 all the time. However, as we walk in reliance on Christ's presence, He says that "I can do all things through Christ who strengthens me!" So, as you compare where you are on the scale to where you want to be, what do you think it would take to move closer to the 10 in each area? (Suggestion: Pick one or two to work on until you move forward to the place where you believe God would have you be. There is something to remember here. It is not about having the right circumstances. So that criteria is off the table).

_____

_____

_____

_____

_____

Day 30

We share resources and rely on God's grace – v. 14-23

Listen to the word –As you listen to the word today, listen for themes of believers sharing their resources.

Read the word- Read Philippians 4:14-23.

The Big Idea

_____

_____

Thoughts, prayers, questions

_____

_____

_____

_____

Memory verse/meditation

_____

Read the brief commentary - In this passage, Paul expresses his appreciation for the sacrificial gifts the Philippians had given him. He encourages them primarily because of the fruit he sees in their lives expressed through their generosity. His particular expression, "a fragrant offering, a sacrifice acceptable and pleasing to God", has its roots in the Old Testament sacrificial system. This was an oft repeated phrase in the book of Leviticus whenever anyone brought a sacrificial offering for sin, restitution, or fellowship. Once these offerings were made, God had these words describe the conclusion. It was fragrant- it was an offering that brought a positive mental, emotional, spiritual, and physical response through the olfactory (smelling) sense. It was an acceptable sacrifice – it had been accepted by God since it had been offered according to God's prescription. It was pleasing to God – this speaks for itself. It brought God's smile and blessing. He also reminds them of his and their ultimate source.

Read the passage again and respond

1. In broad terms, what are the Philippians accomplishing for Paul, a spiritual leader?

    _____

    _____

    _____

    _____

2. How do you think the Philippians responded when they read this section of his letter? Describe it in a few words.

    _____

    _____

    _____

3. What was Paul's comment on reciprocity (mutual sharing and response)?

    _____

    _____

4. What is the significance of the phrase, "according to his riches in glory" which comes after, "my God will meet all your needs..."?

    _____

    _____

    _____

    _____

5. How would you describe the type and depth of the bonds among the believers according to verses 21-23?

    _____

    _____

    _____

Read the passage again and respond.

Principle # 27 - I will give of myself and my resources for the spread of the gospel, trusting God to meet my needs as I rely on His grace.

1. Reflect back on your experience of giving for a cause, a church, an organization you were passionate about and describe the circumstances and how you felt about it.

    _____

    _____

    _____

    _____

2. As we learned from this book, having a heart for giving was a regular practice of the Philippian church. How would you rate yourself in this respect based on the following statements? Check one only.

    a. I practice giving (money, time, energy...) as a lifestyle

        _____

    b. I practice giving regularly with a few gaps (due to).

        _____

    c. I practice giving sporadically, whenever I think about it or am confronted with a compelling need

        _____

    d. I give only when I am drawn in emotionally by specific types of needs (ex. The invisible children of Africa, missionaries pioneering work, Wycliffe Bible translation, rescuing kids being trafficked in US cities, homeless shelters, etc.).

        _____

e. I do not practice giving because (This is not meant to be a judgmental question. Rather, the intent is to help you locate where you are in processing this Christian virtue

_____

_____

_____

f. Wherever you might be in your life with regards to living a giving lifestyle is ok. It is also clear throughout this letter to the Philippians, that as we grow in walking with Christ, we grow in giving of ourselves and our resources. If you believe this is true, then what would your goals be for growth in this area?

1. _____

_____

2. _____

_____

3. _____

_____

4. _____

_____

3. Whom would you like to select as your accountability partner on this?

_____

Notes:

Day 31 – Final Summary

We are at the end of our journey. We have walked through valleys that may have seemed inescapable. We have spent time walking through the fog, not exactly sure where we were going, but holding to one another's hands. We have struggled through the forest chopping brush out of the way, as we moved along at a slower pace. We have camped out in the middle of dark scary places and been comforted by the one who went there before us. We have made a human chain through the rushing water safe to the other side. We have climbed, strained, tugged, pulled, rested, climbed some more, and finally crested the top of the mountain to see the beauty, the truly awesome nature of our Creator-Redeemer. Then we have come back down to the places where we must live out the lessons we have learned, the experiences that have changed us, and the passion to continue the journey. Journey On! Journey on, my brothers and sisters. This life, to which you have been called by Christ Jesus, is truly a journey. It is one that was intended, from first to last, to be done together. There is no such thing as Christian lone rangers. Hopefully, during this journey, that truth has been engraved in your heart.

Summary of Transformation Principles – As you work through these principles in the form of evaluation questions allow God to expose your heart. Reflect on these deeply and record honestly where you are. Celebrate the growth you have made. Acknowledge the areas for greater growth needed. Identify areas where you feel you need help from your spouse, your group, or your spiritual leader. Many intend on growing closer to Christ or to others but do not have a plan for doing so. Years later they are still intending on growing, yet, have not.

You can grow in Christ beyond what you would ever think possible, but it doesn't happen on its own. We are not talking about self-made growth, but simply having a plan to use the means God has provided to grow in Christ in the context of Christian community. So, after this, you have listed the next 7 principles. Use the format provided or your own creation to develop your God-directed plan for growing in Christ in the areas you have identified.

Principle #21 - 4:1-3 - I will pursue unity in Christ by seeking to resolve my relational conflicts and trust Christ with the unresolved.

Am I willing to work through the "messiness" of strained or conflicted relationships? Yes / No / Not sure.

Are there any relationships pending that I need to address?

_____

Relationship(s) in which we seem to be stuck (Philippians 4:1-3)?

_____

How will I deal with these?

_____

_____

Is there any relationship for which I need to seek pastoral or professional assistance?

_____

Principle #22 - 4:4 - I choose today to rejoice in the people, circumstances, gifts, and opportunities given by God.

How would I rate my daily joy level, (i.e., walking in the joy of the Lord as a lifestyle versus being angry, anxious, negative, depressed, and/or etc.) as a lifestyle? 1-2-3-4-5-6-7-8-9-10 (Circle one).

Now, on a separate sheet, and without letting your spouse/bff /significant other/ accountability partner see your response, ask them to rate you.(Give them a concise explanation of the concept of what we mean by joy from the study). 1-2-3-4-5-6-7-8-9-10 (Circle one).

Principle #23 4:5 I am called to maintain a gentle/reasonable disposition in my interactions.

For this one we want to do a comparison like the previous one. We get a more honest picture when we ask for input from people who can be a little more objective. For this one, if you feel comfortable in doing so, select two or three people to give their feedback. Again, to be the most beneficial, do not let them see or know what you or others have indicated at least until afterwards...

Self- rating: 1-2-3-4-5-6-7-8-9-10 Comments:

Person #1: 1-2-3-4-5-6-7-8-9-10 Comments:

Person #2: 1-2-3-4-5-6-7-8-9-10 Comments:

Person #3: 1-2-3-4-5-6-7-8-9-10 Comments:

Principle #24 4:6-7 I will give my anxious thoughts over to God in prayer and anticipate receiving his peace.

What is taking place in your life now that causes you the most anxiety?

_____

_____

How have you been handling it?

_____

_____

How is that working for you?

_____

_____

How might you apply this principle and Scripture truth to this situation?

_____

_____

Principle #25 4:8-9 I choose to meditate on Christ-like virtues and put into practice what I have observed from godly role models.

Are these foundational values a regular part of my perspective in decision making and evaluating relationships? Please respond by circling one:

Always-almost always sometimes seldom almost never never.

Have I begun to implement the focused value-based thinking from the devotional above? Yes/ No/ Not yet but it has been planned/ I still have questions about how it works and need assistance.

Principle #26 4:10-13 I choose to walk in contentment today trusting Christ to provide what he knows I need in each, and every situation.

Briefly describe how you are doing with your contentment level as it relates to your environments.

_____

_____

_____

What are the positive contributing factors?

_____

_____

_____

What are the negative contributing factors?

_____

How can you go from where you are to where you believe God would have you be?

_____

_____

_____

Principle #27 4:14-23 I will give of myself and my resources for the spread of the gospel, trusting God to meet my needs as I rely on His grace.

How am I doing on regular giving? Describe in a few words.

_____

_____

How am I doing on trusting God to meet my needs? Describe in a few words.

_____

Notes:

My Action Plan for Pursuing Growth in Christ (Philippians 3: 13-14 - [13] Brothers, I do not consider that I have made it my own. But one thing I do: forgetting what lies behind and straining forward to what lays ahead, [14] I press on toward the goal for the prize of the upward call of God in Christ Jesus

1. These are the areas of growth in my walk with Jesus. I praise him for them, and I will celebrate these by

    _____

    _____

    _____

    _____

    _____

    These are areas where I have seen some growth but want to see more growth. My plan for continued growth includes: SMART goals = Specific/ Measurable/Action oriented/Realistic/Time limited

    _____

    _____

    _____

    _____

    _____

    These are areas where I feel like I am floundering and if I am truly honest with myself, I need help (we all do in areas of our lives so join the party). This is just a suggestion. Rather than pick a lot of areas why not focus on one for each category. Then, when you feel comfortable with your progress you can always add on to your growth list.

    a. I need help from my spouse/significant other in this area

    _____

    b. I need help from my group/close friends in this area

    _____

    I need help from my spiritual leader/elder/pastor/counselor in this area

    _____

Appendix A – Full List of the Principles

First Leg – Becoming More Self – Aware – Chapter 1 – Sections 1-8

Sections 1-4-Day 2-5

1. Principle #1- v.1, 2 As a servant of Jesus Christ I will submit myself willingly to his lordship and do his will by accessing his limitless resources.
2. Principle #2 v. 3-5 I will develop an ongoing conversation with God for people in my life that is passionate, grateful, confident, and compassionate.
3. Principle #3 v. 6 I choose to stand in God-given confidence that He will complete the work He started in me and people in my life.
4. Principle #4 v. 7-8 I will be passionately supportive of my family, close believers and others God puts in my life.

Sections 5-8-Day 6-9

5. Principle #5 v.9-11 I choose to pray daily for a growing, discerning, decisive love filled with the fruits of Christ's righteousness to the glory of God.
6. Principle #6 v.12-18 I will see adversities as opportunities to advance the gospel through modeling Christ in my response and sharing what makes me different.
7. Principle #7 v. 19-26 Above all else, my purpose in living is Christ, becoming who he wants me to be and doing what he wants me to do.
8. Principle #8 v. 27-30 By faith I accept the eventual reality that living worthy of the gospel will bring the gift of suffering for Christ.

Summary-Day 10

Second Leg Becoming More a Team Player Chapter 2 Sections 1-6

Sections 1-2- Day 11-12(principles 10 and 11 are included on the same day)

9. Principle #9 - 2:1-4 Because of all that God has done for me and because of all the support he has placed around me I choose to be a humble team player and others focused.
10. Principle #10 2:5-8 My settled attitude toward God and for others will be humble obedience to God's will.
11. Principle #11 2:6-11 Like Christ, I will surrender promotion to the Father and look to him for his time and way.

Sections 3-5-Day 13-15

12. Principle #12 2:12-18 Each day I will work out worshipfully in practical living what God has implanted graciously in me.
13. Principle #13 2:19-24 I will seek to be a humble servant of Christ, like Timothy, mentored by a spiritual leader, compassionate, Christ-centered, and of proven character.
14. Principle #14 2:25-30 I commit to give myself unselfishly for the needs of others and to continue growing in relationships.

Summary-Day 16

Third Leg Becoming More Grounded in Christ Chapter 3 Sections 1-6

Sections 1-3-Day 17-19

15. Principle # 15 3:1-6 I will rest in the righteousness of Christ as my source of joy, protection against dilution, and the seal on my heart.
16. Principle #16 3:7-8 I value gaining Christ above all, whatever it may cost, in every situation, context, and relationship.
17. Principle #17 3:9 I release the pursuit of merit-based righteousness in exchange for reliance on the righteousness of Christ.

Sections 4-6-Day 20-22

18. Principle #18 3:10-11 I make it my passion to know Christ experientially, his suffering, his death, and resurrection power.
19. Principle #19 3:12-16 I will pursue with persistence, humility, and growth in Christlikeness.
20. Principle #20 3:17-21 I will follow my models, beware of those who dilute my walk, and wait expectantly for transformation from Christ.

Summary-Day 23

Fourth Leg Becoming More Wholly Connected with Others, Self, and God
Chapter 4 Sections 1-7

Sections 1-4-Day 24-27

21. Principle #21 4:1-3 I will pursue unity in Christ by seeking to resolve my relational conflicts and trust Christ with the unresolvable.
22. Principle #22 4:4 I choose today to rejoice in the people, circumstances, gifts, and opportunities given by God.
23. Principle #23 4:5 I am called to maintain a gentle/reasonable disposition in my interactions with all.
24. Principle #24 4:6-7 I will give my anxious thoughts over to God in prayer and anticipate receiving his peace.

Sections 5-7-Day 28-30

25. Principle #25 4:8-9 I choose to meditate on Christ-like virtues and put into practice what I have observed from godly role models.
26. Principle #26 4:10-13 I choose to walk in contentment today trusting Christ to provide what he knows I need in each situation.
27. Principle #27 4:14-23 I will give of myself and my resources for the spread of the gospel, trusting God to meet my needs as I rely on His grace.

Summary-Day 30

Appendix B – Group Facilitator Guide for a twelve-week Journey

Table of Contents

Introduction

This Group Facilitator Guide provides critical information for facilitating a group that sees actual transformation take place. It is based upon some of the best resources available in both the Biblical and the therapeutic realms. It is also based upon my 45 + years of initiating, facilitating, and multiplying groups. It is also based upon spending 2 decades of training facilitators.

The table of contents lays out where you will find significant suggestions and recommendations for conducting a successful group. The role of the facilitator is the most important ingredient. Who you are as a person is the most critical piece. Introduction and Preparation helps you to set a group atmosphere and structure that fulfills its intended purpose. The suggested format is a workable format that has been used in a wide variety of settings. It provides structure with flexibility. The Journey Overview and components provide specific helps on specific issues. The Group Covenant Foundation provides a rationale for commitment to the Group Covenant. It also provides a worksheet that aids the facilitator in having clarity on the principles involved in the group covenant.

This is important when it comes time to have all the members commit to the Group Covenant before beginning the group. Those who have reservations about committing to the Group Covenant may have their questions addressed. Then, if they remain unable to commit, would not be considered a good fit for the group at this time.

Personal Identification

I can honestly say that I have been where you are, at least for most of you. I have been a college student half-blindly "leading" other college students in prayer, Bible study, witnessing, discipleship, and various other enterprises. I have been an Inner-city Coordinator leading a team of 35 university students on a summer outreach project in upper Manhattan. I have been a church planter who developed a church plant team of multiple personalities, gifts, and motivations who all contributed to planting a church on Manhattan's upper west side. I have been a cell leader in a cell church, facilitated small groups in various church cultures, facilitated the initiation of LIFE groups in new church plants, and developed a comprehensive program that is still running today. I have also facilitated support groups for men pursuing sexual integrity. I continued doing group during the course of completing a master's program for Marriage and Family Therapy with specializations in Sex Therapy and Sexual Addiction Recovery.

I say all of that to relay to you that I probably have a relatively good idea of what you may be thinking and feeling as you get started on this journey. I have attempted to the best of my ability to put myself in your shoes and try to provide a lot of the information, encouragement, and tools that I would have wanted for a transforming journey like this. It can be intimidating in some ways if you are expecting yourself to be the one who does the transforming. However, if you see yourself as an instrument in the hand of God and just be your best self, you will be fine. You will have times of frustration, insecurity, confusion, ambivalence, joy, motivation, and just about everything in between. Draw from your leaders, your peers, and your support network, as well as those you seek to lead. You will find strength you did not realize was available.

Let me offer this as an encouragement. My passion is to see lives transformed by the power of the gospel. I have discovered over forty-nine years of being a follower of Christ that God uses many ways and means to transform lives. However, as always, His plan and method is to use men and women who are yielded to him. Even the therapeutic community has discovered that the single most significant factor in effective therapy/transformation is the therapist (or in your case, the facilitator) himself/herself. So, it is with great confidence that I offer the following suggestions to help you facilitate/lead a successful group.

This leader/facilitator guide provides some general direction for those who sense a calling and/or are selected to facilitate these Personal and Relational Transformation groups. By virtue of its very name, this type of group is designed in every way to provide opportunities to experience change personally and relationally. Expect personal transformation as well as being a tool to help others see their lives transformed.

Role of the Group Facilitator

In your own creative way, you will want to communicate clearly your role to your group members. It will feel good to have people look up to and depend upon you. We all understand that. Allowing them to become dependent on you, however, will be the temptation that you need to resist. The way in which you can best serve your group members is to empower them. You will constantly be working yourself out of a job.

As a large part of your role is to model, a great portion of that is done by the type of atmosphere that you establish with the group at the onset. Group cohesion is critical to the development and experiential growth of the group. If you implement the following guidelines, you will see the group propelled into a number of life change experiences. As you proceed through each leg of the journey seek to maintain a growth-rich atmosphere and you will see wonderful things take place.

When there is an accepting affirming atmosphere there is tremendous potential for personal and group growth. Seek to foster that accepting atmosphere by modeling and facilitating these four values: Absolute worth, autonomy, accurate empathy, and affirmation. Absolute worth values each person for the person of inherent value and worth whom God created them to be. "After God completed his creation on the sixth day, He saw all that he created and said, it was very good" (Genesis 1:31).

A second very important aspect of acceptance is accurate empathy. This is where we set aside our preconceived notions, our own ideas, listen to the other person, and try to see from their own unique perspective. When we do this, group members will sense that we "get" them and will be more inclined to be open and authentic. As each person feels accepted and safe enough to open up, it will encourage others to do the same.

Next, a critical component of genuine acceptance is recognizing that each person is autonomous. Each person has the irrevocable right and capacity of self-direction. Some may refer to this as free will or free moral agency. When we sincerely honor and respect each person's autonomy, we validate them and motivate them to take ownership for their lives. As you seek to respect and model this quality in your group, you will stimulate a great deal of openness and creativity. As the group grows in practicing this trait mutually, you will see greater group cohesion and comradery.

Finally, affirmation is the fourth aspect of acceptance. Seek and acknowledge each person's strengths and efforts. Find excuses to praise. Think about your own motivation. Would you rather be encouraged with your strengths and efforts or criticized and judged by what you had not done. As you model these four aspects of acceptance it will foster a group atmosphere that practices these values.

The facilitator's role, just as the name is defined, is to facilitate. It is critical to the initiation, development, and interpersonal growth of the group. It is not a teaching, preaching, counseling, or mentoring role. It is first, foremost, and throughout an opportunity to facilitate personal and relational transformation. You are a tool in the hand of the Great Transformer God. The primary way in which this is done is by modeling how to walk the journey. You will also assist group members to walk the journey by showing them how to use the same tools you have used in your journey. You will help create a safe, affirming, and caring group environment (see Group Covenant page 97). You will also want to be able to access available counseling/church staff when appropriate. They will provide for you the proper channels for accessing your counseling center/church resources. This guide helps provide some practical pointers for helping you accomplish the purpose of facilitating life transformation. Other appendices provide other resources for this purpose as well. Please review all the material to be aware of all the resources available to you. This will be especially important if you have not yet been involved in a group that progressed through the various stages of growth and multiplication. It is strongly suggested for every Facilitator, and especially for those less experienced that you take time to read and revisit the Group Life Cycle in Appendix D.

Introduction and Preparation for the Journey

The first gathering of the group is not part of the 12 weeks journey. It is a preparatory meeting where the tone, atmosphere, direction, and commitment for participating in the group should be clearly articulated. It is also an opportunity for those participating to be able to have their questions about the journey clarified (In appendix G you will find frequently asked questions in preparation for this time of Q and A).

- Biblical Rationale (As provided in the introduction and in appendix C). Page 1 and 2 of the Introduction provides a general biblical rationale including Scripture references as a source of personal transformation. Appendix C provides extensive Scripture references for the purposes, relationships, atmosphere, and goals of these group transformation experiences. It is recommended that group facilitators/leaders become very familiar with the significance of these passages.
- It is also recommended that during the introductory session, a Biblical and Dynamic Foundation is established since they are both the why and the how of this journey. This will provide a solid starting point for the participants. A suggested conceptual outline follows. Use your creativity sensitive to the learning styles of your group. What you will want to do is just cover these 2 points in a brief survey fashion. You could make a Bible study series out of each, however, that is not the purpose here. Use your creativity in communicating these critical truths.
- Suggested Outline for Biblical Rationale

You may want to develop these:

o   Personal Transformation- Obviously there is no "magic" formula that produces transformation. However, these Biblical truths are transformational. They are God's absolutes and when followed passionately you can expect to experience change.

- Meditation on the word brings prosperity and success as defined by God Joshua 1:8.
- Meditation on the word daily creates fruitfulness and prosperity Psalm 1:1-3.
- Too many blessed benefits to put here Psalm 119.
- We present our bodies as living sacrifices and he transforms us by renewing our minds according to God's will Romans 12:1-2.
- God's clearly defined will is that we be filled with the Spirit, resulting in joyfulness, mutual encouragement, and mutual submissiveness Ephesians 5:17-21.
- God's word living in us gives us wisdom for living Colossians 3:16.
- God's word is all sufficient to equip us completely for serving him 2 Timothy 3:14-17.
- God's word is not mere language, rather, it is a living entity that penetrates the soul Hebrews 4:11-13.
- The promise for doers of the word James 1:21-25.

o   Relational Transformation - Small groups who met from house to house in the book of Acts were transformed as they interacted with one another in community. They were a microcosm of the larger church community and included all the functions and purposes of the larger church community. The following are just a few of the lifestyle concepts and relational principles which are a vital part of Christian community groups. These comprise the fertile environment in which personal and relational transformation takes place. The atmosphere then is a place where followers of Christ:

- Honor one another Romans 12:10
- Accept one another Romans 15:7
- Look out for one another 1 Corinthians 10:24

118

- Carry one another's burdens Galatians 6:1
- Forgive one another Ephesians 4:32
- Submit to one another Ephesians 5:21
- Look out for one another's interests Philippians 2:4
- Bear with one another Colossians 3:13
- Love one another 1 Thessalonians 4:9
- Meet with and encourage one another Hebrews 10:25
- Confess your sins to one another James 5:16
- Offer hospitality to one another 1 Peter 4:9
- Have fellowship with one another 1 John 1:7

    o These passages would be a good place to revisit from time to time to keep the journey in perspective (see appendix C for a full list). Our journey of transformation is very much a personal journey, but it is also a journey made in the context of a caring Christian community. These two cannot be separated without it affecting the outcome.

- Learning styles (Introduction page 4. Attempts have been made to appeal to all 5 senses as well as cognitive, affective, behavioral, and relational aspects of our personalities. One of the best ways to facilitate learning and growth is by modeling and demonstration from your previous experience).
- Components of the journey tools (Introduction pages 5, 6. More will be said about these tools in the following pages). It is highly recommended that each group facilitator participates in one of these Personal and Relational Transformation Journeys prior to leading one, especially since so much rides on modeling. This will prepare the group facilitator/leader to be able to communicate clearly and passionately during the introductory session. This will also prepare him or her to be more confident in facilitating a group. Group facilitator training in a condensed model will be made available for those with sufficient experience. This concept adheres to the principle that more is caught than taught.

Suggested Group Format

- 8-12 People Maximum- This is to allow proper time for each person to be able to participate in a significant way and to allow for significant group events during the group time.
- Time frame It is strongly recommended to allow for a minimum of one and a half hours (1.5 hours) to allow for enough time to cover pertinent Bible content in a sufficient manner, adequate time for group processing of individual work, and the inclusion of prayer and worship.
- Format

  o 15 minutes-Warm Up time- fellowship/announcements
  o 5 minutes Worship/heart preparation utilizing the suggested worship songs in a CD or streaming format, live, or an alternative, such as, reading a Psalm, other Scripture passage, the practice of mindfulness after the reading of Scripture, or practicing silence. This portion can vary as needs are apparent and the Spirit leads.
  o 20 minutes- Scripture Understanding Focus- This segment of the time focuses on the following components: Listen to the word, Read the word, the Big Idea, Thoughts, prayers, questions, Verses for memorization/meditation. The group facilitator may want to do a brief context introduction, set the interactive atmosphere, or set the focus for the how the Bible will be discussed. The main idea is to allow for time in an open and accepting atmosphere where each member can share their exploration/discovery results and their remaining questions. This is not a time to have a huge debate or to get into a theological argument. The focus is on understanding clearly what you are each seeking to apply that will potentially change your life in significant ways. It is sort of observation and interpretation by committee. Be careful to start out in a disciplined manner. Stick to the time. Stick to the purpose. Further questions beyond 20 minutes can be addressed personally or after the formal time is over. Remember to set proper precedents.
  o 40 minutes- Life Transformation Focus- This portion is the ultimate focus of the whole journey. This section includes the following: Read the passage the second time and respond- application, read the

passage the third time and respond-principle, and the summary of transformation principles after each leg of the journey. We do the Scripture focus well so that we may apply God's truth appropriately. We make personal application in the context of a caring community who both supports us and keeps us accountable in positive ways.

o   10 minutes Prayer and Wrap up At first thought you may get the idea that prayer is not important in this process. You would be thinking wrong. It is so important that it is recommended prior to the group, all throughout working through the material individually and in group, afterwards in this 10 minute group segment, and whenever deemed appropriate, as a welcomed and passionately embraced "interruption". One way to "pray without ceasing" is to implement the Jesus Prayer. See the appendix for this.

The Journey Overview

It is especially important for the group facilitator to set the tone at the beginning of this journey for all the elements involved. During the introductory session, you'll want to accentuate the importance of starting out right by clarifying what is involved in each component of this journey – listening to the word, reading the word (big ideas, thoughts, prayers, questions, memorization/meditation), reading the brief commentary, reading the passage and responding, and reading the passage along with the principle and application. All along the way it is especially important to get feedback from those participating so that there is clarity, understanding, and maximum buy-in. This will ensure the highest level of motivation for continuing the journey to its completion.

The general flow of the journey is to start out with more instructions and gradually reduce them less and less so that those on the journey are gaining confidence and operating more and more from an autonomous base although mutually interdependent in the group. A large part of this journey involves self-discovery of truth rather than having it spoon-fed to the group member. The group facilitator will be a key to ensuring this goal. You are there to facilitate learning, discovery, and personal growth, not to make members dependent on you. Usually, when members have questions, it will be better to ask them how they would address the issues rather than giving them a direct answer.

You can also redirect to allow the group to address the issue raised. You must use your discretion here, but, generally speaking, help them to help themselves find answers rather than merely giving the answers to them.

A good model to follow in your role as facilitator would be to: teach, train, model, and release. Gradually, you will teach less and less until you stop teaching, training less and less until you stop training, and finally, merely model. This process can be somewhat individual specific. We recognize that not everyone has the same motivational level, the same personality, the same learning style, or the same spiritual growth level. So, in your application of these general guidelines, seek to be sensitive to the Holy Spirit's direction. If you have specific questions, consult your pastoral or leadership staff.

The general approach to Scripture in this personal and relational transformation experience is first to properly and thoroughly exegete the text to ascertain its meaning in context as well as its significance. Subsequently, modern-day relevancy and application is made. The same is true with the design of this journey.

Notes:

Components for the Journey

At the beginning of each week there is an introduction to the biblical passage that sets the context for the remaining study/journey. As the purpose of this journey is not a thorough biblical study, these introductions are intentionally brief. For those who are deep Bible students, appendix F includes an extensive Bible and ministry resource list.

At the beginning of each day there is a very brief introduction to put the day's biblical text in context. Sometimes this has to do with the historical background. Sometimes it is more personal, or application driven in its orientation. Following that section: Listen to the Word includes an opportunity for the person to interact with the text personally. This is intentionally placed before the brief commentary so that it will encourage self-discovery and autonomy in one's approach to the Scriptures. We are not seeking to produce Bible scholars; however, we are seeking to teach people how to get into the word for themselves. You, the group facilitator/leader, can be a great catalyst in this. We are seeking to foster Christ-followers who have inquisitive minds, are open and honest in their personal application of and reaction to truth, are okay with having questions about their faith, and are consistent in pursuing the truth. It is important to record their discoveries because this enables them to process the truth. Also included in this section is the section: Read the brief commentary. It is important to encourage them to do the prior section before reading the brief commentary. It may be a temptation to do the brief commentary first so that they have the "correct" answers. What is important is that they process this for themselves first before reading the commentary. Then they may seek confirmation if they so desire after first digging on their own. Please encourage them to do this as otherwise it will create a dependency upon the commentary as opposed to self-discovery.

In the section, "Read the selected passage again and answer the questions", the questions are more content specific and seek to get at understanding the meaning and the significance of the passage. Sometimes personal relevancy is included. Again, it is important that each member record their findings: 1. First and foremost it is a part of the transformational process. 2. It provides a basis for group discussion.

The next section: "Read the word for the third time and respond to these two questions"; seeks to apply the truth stated in a principle and to share the discovery with someone. These two components are essential for the transformation process. Knowing truth and understanding it is very important. Applying truth is essential for life transformation. In addition, sharing your experience of the life transforming truth is also a very important part of the transforming process. It does two things. First, it confirms this truth in your own heart and mind and begins to "reprogram" the thought processes and emotional processes. Secondly, sharing this with another encourages both you and those in your caring Christian community to continue on the journey.

Following, I have provided suggestions for each leg of the journey. The organization of this material is as follows. The first leg, Becoming More Self Aware is associated with chapter 1 and so on. The suggestions in this section are going to be oriented to personal growth and development, group processing, and community development.

First, I would like to make some general suggestions about facilitating these transformational groups. The overall focus is to have a transformational experience, not merely a Bible study. Therefore, although part of the discussion, of necessity, must be content oriented, the majority of the group interaction should be application oriented and have an internal focus rather than an objective focus. How does one help facilitate this? Know the group members and know how to elicit responses and stimulate interactions among members. Part of this happens through a wise use of a variety of questions.

Closed ended questions will be used primarily for gaining specific answers. Some of these questions would anticipate a yes or no answer. Other questions of this type would be seeking very concrete answers. These are not the questions best equipped for stimulating discussion and interaction. These questions should be targeted. They should also be limited to understanding the biblical text and specific questions in the material.

Open-ended questions facilitate discussion, deeper sharing (eliciting greater self-awareness and responsiveness to others), application, and group interaction. Some examples follow.

1. How did that passage impact your thinking... feeling... experience...?
2. As you read this passage what were some of your thoughts, feelings, reactions, questions...?
3. How do you see yourself putting this into practice?
4. As you read about Paul, Timothy, Epaphroditus how do you think they may have felt in the situation? How do you think you would have felt given your current spiritual state?

5. How would you rate yourself on this scale?

6. As you reflect on God's perspective of you, how does that make you feel? What does it stir you to think? How does it motivate you to want to interact with your wife, children, family, or others?

7. What is happening with you as you hear_____ (fill in a name from your group) share what he did? What would you like to be able to do for him/her or how would you like to be able to respond to her/him?

Your role as a facilitator will be to help group members come to an accurate understanding of the text so that the application of the truth is most appropriate. Part of that has to do with your knowledge and preparation. Another part of reaching that goal is contingent upon how you elicit group members to share their discovery of the meaning and significance of the texts. Remember, your end goal is to work yourself out of a job. Equip them to be able to interact with the text, the questions provided, and one another so that eventually they will not need you. A huge part of accomplishing that task has to do with how effective you are in getting the group members to interact with one another.

The "Journey by Leg" lays out a 12 Week journey after the initial orientation and Group Covenant signing on the Introduction Day.

The Journey by Leg

This section of the appendix provides suggestions, ideas, hints, questions, practical wisdom on specific sections of the Journey by leg. Some of it is content based. Some of it is process based. Some of it is interpersonal dynamics based. Some of it is group process oriented. It is meant to give you a "heads up "concerning some of the individual and group "stuff" that comes up and is provided only as one source of potential help. When necessary, always seek the help of your spiritual leaders or counselors.

- First Leg Becoming More Authentic and Self-Aware Philippians 1 Sections 1-8-(Day 2-10)

    o Sections 1-4 (Week 1-Days 2-5)
    o Sections 5-8 (Week 2-Days 6-9)
    o Summary (Week 3-Day 10)

- Second Leg Becoming More of a Team Player Philippians 2 Sections 1-5- (Day 11-16)

  o Sections 1-3 (Week 4-Days 11-13)
  o Sections 4-5 (Week 5-Days 14-15)
  o Summary (Week 6-Day 16)

- Third Leg Becoming More Grounded in Christ Philippians 3 Sections 1-6- (Day 17-23)

  o Sections 1-3 (Week 7-Day 17-19)
  o Sections 4-6 (Week 8-Day 20-22)
  o Summary (Week 9-Day 23)

- Fourth Leg Becoming More Wholly Connected with Others, Self, and God - Philippians 4 Sections 1-7-(Day 24-30)

  o Sections 1-4 (Week 10-Day 24-27)
  o Sections 5-7 (Week 11-Day 28-30)
  o Summary (Week 12-Day 31)

Group Facilitator Notes:

- First Leg Becoming More Authentic and Self-Aware Philippians 1 Sections 1-8 (Week 1-3, Day 2-10)

The theme for the first leg has more to do with application than it does the actual meaning of the text. The truth is, before one can interact effectively with others, he or she must become more authentic and self -aware, God -centered, and emotionally attuned to others. As you look at the first section and reflect on the overall focus that Paul provides, it is not difficult to see that there is a blending of the three areas mentioned above. Paul and Timothy saw themselves as servants in their relationship with the Philippians. They exhibited attributes of humility, compassion, perseverance, and passion on behalf of their fellow believers. They encouraged them to pray passionately for one another. They also had learned to view themselves and others from God's perspective (verse 6). This influences both thinking and feeling. This chapter also calls each partner in the gospel to follow Paul's model of enduring suffering, serving others for Christ, and living lives that reflect the Gospel's impact. Ask yourself this question. How do I facilitate members of the group understanding, experiencing, and practicing these values?

A critical piece which will determine how your group progresses has to do with the extent to which they accept and apply the four key values mentioned under the Journey Overview – absolute worth, acceptance, autonomy, and affirmation. The more your group members practice these values in relationship with one another the greater cohesiveness and depth of participation will take place. As a facilitator, you need to have this question on your back burner: to what extent do I see these core values evident in our group? A follow-up question then, would be, how do I encourage even more of this to happen?

Take enough time for each group member to share their expectations, goals, reservations, fears, and doubts. You want to create a safe, accepting atmosphere where these things can be shared and processed without judgment, criticism, or comparison. God is big enough to handle them. It does not mean you have to agree. What it does mean, is that the group accepts the person where they are and does not require them to step up to where they "should be" before entrance into the group. We accept individuals where they are so that we can join them in their journey forward.

o Sections 1-4 (Week 1-Day 2-5))

The key word for this first section is precedents. It is important to begin well. It sets the pace, the tone, and the expectation for the rest of the journey. A key factor in developing a group that grows together and goes deeper together hinges upon establishing a safe and accepting environment. A huge part of that developing is contingent upon individual participation. A great part of honoring autonomy is highlighting individual responsibility. What that means in terms of this journey, is that each person needs to do the work before showing up. That means following the instructions in the journey guideline, listening to the word, working through the questions, and coming prepared to group. It is important to remember that each person and the group only derive benefits from this journey to the extent that they invest in it. Small investment equals small returns. Great investment equals great returns. Will there be times in which someone has legitimate reasons for not having prepared? Yes, but we all have the same amount of time in a day and a week. Part of your group selection procedure should be to identify those who have the time and are willing to make a commitment to the group and the process.

The group should agree on a mutual standard of expectation with agreed-upon exceptions and then stick to it. This will help to ensure the maximum participation. This would be in addition to the Group Contract, which the group has had the opportunity to read, discuss, and sign. For most of us, the natural tendency would be to gloss over this. Please do not make that mistake. It would cause ripple effects on your group. Balance is a key concept here. Remember, when Jesus came into this world, he brought grace and truth. Yes, it is not always clear where the line is. It also is an uncomfortable place to be, especially if you have a difficult time holding people accountable. The best approach here is model, teach, train, release. If the group will commit to the process, then each one has a role in holding each other accountable in a positive way.

The first week, it will be important to address all questions related to how the individual responsibility works, how the group dynamics work, and whatever form of communication you set up on an ongoing basis. Some groups establish accountability partners. Some use email and texting accountability. Each group needs to create its own parameters for effective ongoing interaction.

Another very simple but easily overlooked attitude and practice is essential for this journey to be beneficial to each member. In order to be authentic, it is important to be honest with oneself. Therefore, as members answer the questions about themselves in response to the word, it is critical that they answer as they actually are and not as they feel they should be. If you have established an atmosphere of safety and acceptance, members will be much more inclined to be honest with each other.

o   Sections 5-8 (Week 2-Day 6-9)

Listen to the Word A great part of the transformation journey involves becoming more aware and accustomed to God's ways with us. As we do become more aware of God's ways, we learn to make direction adjustments to him and his guidance. We begin to discern his guidance as we learn how to listen truly to his Spirit's voice. You can play a vital role in your group's sensitivity to God's Spirit by modeling the principles in these experience-oriented exercises and by showing them how as well.

Day 5 Read and Respond I would like to provide just a note for this area. Sometimes, if a member is really dealing with issues in his relationships, he may experience emotions or thoughts that are troubling. This is not an uncommon experience, nor cause for alarm. This is an opportunity for the group to rally in support (not offer unrequested advice) and encouragement. It is critical for you, the facilitator, to be aware of the abilities and limitations that the group presents when someone is in distress. If you determine that this member's needs are beyond your group's capacity to meet, seek pastoral or counselor assistance.

Day 6 Two excellent resources for growing in one's prayer life include John MacArthur's book on the Lord's prayer – Alone with God and David Benner's book, Opening to God. These references are listed in

Appendix E – Basic Bible resources. They each approach the subject of prayer very differently. John MacArthur provides an exegetical and practical commentary on the model prayer that Jesus taught his disciples. MacArthur includes many practical principles for growing in your prayer life. Benner, on the other hand, approaches prayer from four ancient traditions concerning how to pray referred to as Lectio Divina. His is a more creative and flexible format that can stimulate a different approach to praying. This may be especially helpful for those who have a difficult time practicing this discipline. Again, this journey emphasizes the experience of a life altering transformation. All outside resources should be used only as aids to better facilitate this objective.

Read the Passage again and Respond Scales are tools provided to help members become a little more concrete in evaluating their spiritual walks. The purpose of the scales is to help members have an honest assessment of where they see themselves in practicing spiritual disciplines. This is intended to be a means of becoming more self-aware in their spiritual journey. It is also a potential means of motivation and goal setting for where they want to go in their journey. There will be a variety of scales utilized throughout the journey. Each time a scale is used, a brief explanation is provided so members have a better understanding of how to use it. The important thing to remember with the scales is that they are tools, a means to an end, and not the end. Part of the difficulty in any kind of spiritual or emotional growth is that the means for evaluating growth tends to be very subjective and therefore not very accurate or helpful. The scales help make this a bit more concrete and accessible. If they help members do that, they have met their purpose.

Day 7 The work that members do for this day has the potential for creating a need for more time to share and process in group. It would be advisable to allow each one to share after you set an allotted amount of time for each. If there are special circumstances that reasonably require more time for a member, it may be helpful to bring that before the group to determine what to do. Then, everyone will have time to share, and you will be able to handle special circumstances. Also, be on the lookout for those members who may be "oblivious" to time or the needs of others to share. Tactfully, limit that person's time for sharing. Otherwise, if someone is allowed to dominate the time of the group, it will adversely affect group cohesiveness and hinder the journey.

Principle #7 Question 2 This is just a reminder before a member selects someone to share his experience with someone other than a group member. Encourage group members to evaluate carefully with whom it is appropriate to share their personal stuff. It may be helpful to process this during group time before they do so with someone outside of the group. What is most important is that whomever they share their journey with should be someone safe, accepting, and able to keep confidentiality to an appropriate level.

Day 9 Read the Passage again and Respond If you are highly motivated, it might be helpful to scan the gospel of Mark (only 16 chapters) for "markers" that describe how Jesus lived as a model we should follow. This, of course, would focus on his example as the model man, not his divinity.

o Summary (Week 3–Day 10)

The Summary of Transformation Principles located at the beginning of Day 10, provides an opportunity to pull all the principles together in one place. Part of the point of this is obviously for review. It is also an opportunity for both individual and group review of the content, the individual learning experience, the group interaction, and especially the practical application of the life transforming truths found in Philippians. Most importantly, this is an opportunity to establish a strong base for ongoing transformation.

As a facilitator, you will want to set the tone and expectation for making this section as mutually and individually beneficial as possible. Here are a few suggestions for making that possible.

1. Encourage members to take time to reflect, pray, think, and remember their journey so far.

2. Encourage members to ask others (group members, spouses, peers, family, fellow believers, etc.) how they see their own application of each principle.

3. Yes, you all have a week to work on this intentionally. It is recommended that you work possibly only on one or two principles per day, allow enough time to reflect, pray, and ask others, and to Journal. The point of this is that it takes time to internalize and incorporate these principles into your lifestyle. Encourage your group members to take this seriously and not to hurriedly jot down answers right before coming to group. Here's a thought. Some groups establish a rule. If you do the work, you get to share, if you do not, you may be present but not share. Make it a group decision if you would like to do it. That way, everyone is on the same page.

4. Encourage your members, after reflecting, praying, and asking others to set up their individual action plan, to implement a growth game plan.

During the group time, you will want to provide opportunity for the group to do the following:

1. Celebrate their areas of growth.
2. Evaluate/share honestly where they are individually (this can be done because the group has established itself as a safe, accepting, and encouraging environment).
3. Share areas where members feel they need the help of others and how they plan to access help.
4. Determine areas in which pastoral or counselor help is required. Use your discretion. You may want to recommend to the member to seek this assistance privately depending on the situation and context. Consult with your spiritual leader for wisdom and discernment in this area.

- Second Leg Becoming More of a Team Player Philippians 2 Sections 1-5(Week 4-6, Day 11-16)

Take some time to ask yourself the question, to what extent does this group feel, think, act, and interact like a team? How would I describe this group in terms of it being a team? How would I communicate this to my group to encourage more of the team building? What kind of things could I do, suggest, or facilitate to help build team cohesiveness?

Then ask, what are the group's strengths for building a team atmosphere? Who are the leaders in that area? How are they doing the team building? How can I empower them more? Then ask, what are our weaknesses? (This is not a character question, rather, it is a functional one. Let's make sure we address function and not people's character. I mention this because sometimes it is easy to get these confused). What members seem to be struggling with being part of the team? How can I or someone in the group best come alongside them to encourage them to integrate more into the group team atmosphere? What help do I need from my spiritual leader or pastor?

  o Sections 1-2 (Week 4, Day 11-12)

    It is one thing to memorize the verses, know them by heart, and be able to quote them verbatim. This is good. However, it alone comes short of life transformation and experiential knowledge of Jesus Christ. The question with which you want to wrestle is, "How do I facilitate the group experiencing these truths"? How may I help facilitating and attitude that follows the model of Christ in serving others? What acts of service might we get the group involved with to put this into practice?

    Read the word These statements in vs. 1,2 are great "affirmation statements" to repeat daily in front of the bathroom mirror or in the car driving to work. This would be especially true if you had someone in your group who has recently stepped out of line and feels guilty, ashamed, or distant. It may also be beneficial for someone experiencing a low opinion of themselves.

Day 12-v. 5-11 There might be a real temptation with this passage, to gravitate to an intellectual or theological debate. This might be especially true if you have a Bible College or seminary trained group member. It is recommended that this type of discussion remain limited and referred to pastoral leaders. It is not that the discussion would not be a valid thing. The point is that the practical nature of this transformation journey could be ill-affected if the discussion becomes too theoretical/philosophical. You must know your group's abilities and limitations.

Read the passage again You will have people at different levels in their spiritual journey. It may be that some have difficulty "getting really personal" with God. Encourage them to be painfully honest and speak to God as they would their most trusted friend or family member. For some, you may need to give them some practical pointers on how to do this. For others, it may be that their view of God has been skewed by the model of an authority figure who misused their position or who was not spiritually mature. You may want to find in a more mature group member to pair with them or refer them to one of your spiritual leaders.

o   Sections 3-5 (Week 5-Day 13-15)

Day 13-Read Brief Commentary-Encourage the group members in this by modeling it yourself and modeling an inquisitiveness in your group meetings.

Day 14-Memory/meditation verse-Remember at the beginning, we stated that the comments instruction and suggestions would begin to taper off somewhat. This is an example.

Day 15 –Your thoughts, prayers, and questions Do not let your group members miss some of these subtle changes. We all have tendencies to move quickly past those things that look familiar. Encourage them to assume each day will have its own unique qualities.

Read passage again and respond –In order to facilitate growth, development, and progress, it may be necessary to nudge gently those who tend to be content-only oriented, very theoretical, unmotivated, or "too busy". These may be excuses for not seeking to implement change but are not very good reasons.

Read the passage again and respond I know you may already know this and practice it routinely. If you do, wonderful, keep up the good work. But, for those of you who are more spontaneous, creative, or flexible (or however you describe yourself)., it is very good to follow up periodically on your group members to see how they are doing with what they committed to do by way of practical application.

o Summary (Week 6, Day 16)

Summary of transformation principles Remind your group members that the summary week is not a vacation week. It is more of an intensive application week. Review preview weeks, gain allies, and put it into practice. Elicit others, who you can trust, to assist you in your journey and tell you what they really think when you ask for their evaluation.

Action Plan It is critical that you build on each group member's strengths. This will encourage them even more. It will also motivate them to continue to persevere when times get tough. It will also enable them to endure their challenges and not become discouraged when things do not go the way planned. This is an ongoing process, which, if practiced throughout the group journey, will become personal practices for them once the group has concluded.

Touch base with each person in your group periodically to be aware of growth in his/her life. More importantly, you will be aware of those areas in which they are struggling earlier on in the process. This will enable you to be more helpful for them and refer them earlier on in the process. Continue to create a safe, growth -oriented atmosphere. When you must go outside of the group, it will be more natural and less of a battle.

- Third Leg Becoming More Grounded in Christ Philippians 3 Sections 1-6, Week 7-9, Day 17-23

This section is close-up and personal. Part of what you may want to ask yourself prior to this leg is, where are my group members in their overall relationship with Christ? Where are they in relationship to each of the values represented in days 17- 23? Where are each of my group members in relationship to the extent they rely upon Christ's righteousness? Where are each of my group members as he relates to valuing gaining Christ over everything? Where are they concerning releasing their own self-righteousness to receive God's gift of righteousness? Are they living by grace or still seeking to merit a relationship with Christ? To what extent are they doing either? Is there a passion to know Christ experientially or is there a satisfaction with a casual knowledge of Christ? Do my group members see pursuing Christ a lifelong relationship journey or more of a pragmatic thing that Christians are supposed to do? Are my group members watching out for people or things which would dilute God's truth in their lives? How do I facilitate having a safe atmosphere to explore where they are? How do I help them identify where they are and move forward? Of course, all these questions presume that you have begun to work through them. You are still in the journey and are not required to have everything together to lead and facilitate. That is the beauty of being in a group. All of you are on the journey and can learn from one another. Modeling a teachable spirit in a humble heart will infect others.

o Sections 1-3 (Week 7, Day 17-19)

Day 17 is important to celebrate each positive thing, each step forward. Some make huge strides. Some make baby steps. Each person moves ahead at his or her own rate. As the group celebrates each person's progress, it will help fuel the courage to make bolder changes. Some groups have set up specific occasions for a time of celebration and fellowship (something on the order of a "mini-awards banquet".

Listen to the Word You may want to take a little time to do some "holy visualization". Imagine being there. What does it look like? How do you feel when Jesus takes the scroll? What thoughts go through your mind?

Read the passage again and respond to the questions Sometimes we get "stuck" in the habit of responding to circumstances in a negative, pessimistic, or critical manner and it just becomes "second nature". We have tendencies to "visualize" a negative outcome. Here is a thought. Maybe it would be helpful to get your group to "brainstorm" positive responses to those circumstances which test them.

Day 18 Listen to the Word Ask the group members to share what God's messages have been to them.

Day 19 There is a huge battle, for many believers, whether it is due to church culture, personal values, or family perspectives over the perceived need to earn, merit, or win God's favor. This then, can become a major struggle in the group member's personal walk with the Lord. If the established attitude is one that seeks to earn God's favor for his grace, mercy, forgiveness, and life then an unattainable goal has been established. Remember the standard of the law? He who offends in one point is guilty of all. As a group facilitator, it is critical to help your group members understand and experience grace. It is God's gift of freedom that enables us to establish healthy boundaries. If you are wrestling personally in this area, you may want to consult one of your spiritual leaders or pastors. Of course, as a model of vulnerability and authenticity, and if the group has been established as a safe place to do so, you may want to share your own experience with them.

o   Sections 4-6 (Week 8, Day 20-22)

Day 20

Partners in the gospel... know Christ experientially...

Experientially... What does that mean for you? Think it through/feel it through/how does it affect your physical state? (Say what?) We serve Christ with our physical senses and the rest of our body. Romans

6:6, 11, 13, 16 articulate this clearly. We must intellectually know something (v.6). The old man was crucified that the "body of sin" – flesh might be destroyed. It is not the body, that is evil. It is what we do with it that becomes good or evil. We do not want to fulfill the flesh, but we do want to use our bodies appropriately to serve Christ. Consider (v. 11) asks us to use our God given judgment (intellect/emotions/will) to be dead to sin but alive to God. Yield (v. 13) instructs us to surrender our members (bodily parts) as instruments (or more accurately, weapons) to God and for righteous acts. Therefore, with our eyes, ears, noses, mouths, and skin we are to serve God. You may want to ask your group members some of the same questions from above and to get them to think about and respond to how they serve Christ through their bodies. This helps to make the relationship with Christ more concrete and not merely in their heads.

Read the passage and respond.

This section may be difficult for some group members on a number of levels. If closeness in relationships, in general, is a struggle, then it should be of no surprise that a relationship with Christ is as well. However, if each member will be as open, honest, transparent as they feel safe to be, this could open new avenues of closeness with Christ and other believers. There is no progress without obedience. There is no obedience without trust. There is no trust without risk. There is no risk without taking the first step. You may want to prep the group in a previous group time for what is coming and revisit your "safety policies". As a practical matter, and you may also want to have Kleenexes available.

Day 21

Read the word.

It is his love letter to you. As a practical note, you may want to share experiences of receiving "love" letters from your spouse's either before marriage or afterwards. The more specific experiences you can elicit the better. It makes the experience more concrete and highlights the concrete way in which God's love letter touches us in our experience.

Meditation/memory verses:

This might be a good time to check in with the group members and get feedback on how the memorization and meditation is going. Again, since the whole tenor of the group is oriented to model first, it may be a good idea to demonstrate this benefit by modeling it. Example: "during my quiet time, I memorized this verse and then during the day I had this experience. I found this verse to be very comforting, challenging, instructive, you fill in the blank".

Read passage and respond.

It Is very important that the questions which asked the group members to evaluate where they are in specific areas of their journey with Christ, be addressed thoughtfully without rushing through the. This will be the most beneficial for the individual member and the group as each person shares where they are in their journey. At times, it may be difficult, especially for those who feel they have been failing more than victorious. It is important that the group provide a safe atmosphere for them to grow.

Day 22

Here is a thought. If it would be appropriate for the group culture, maybe you could share your favorite crime busters from Criminal Minds, CSI, Elementary, Law and Order, or some other crime show. You Could Talk about How They Solve the Crime. Then you could relate it to how your group can be on the lookout for people, programs, or processes which tend to dilute the truth in your lives.

Principle #20

This section provides a tremendous opportunity for the facilitator/ group leader to create a healthy environment for change. It also provides the group a tremendous opportunity to be able to discuss the diversions, distractions, discouragements, and disagreeable people who have negative influences in your walk with Christ. It is critical that the safe and accepting atmosphere be maintained to help individual group members move from unhealthy friendships with bad influences, to more healthy Christlike relationships. Most of us, if not all, have experienced situations in which we have observed or have heard about our children, our friends, or workplace associates being impacted by destructive influences. We have wanted to help. However, it has become evident that they are unresponsive to our input. We do not want that to happen in group. This is where we put the four values, mentioned at the beginning of the study, into practice absolute worth, autonomy, affirmation, and accurate empathy. These are four aspects of genuine acceptance. As group members share their experience, we provide a safe and non-judgmental place for them to do that. We also rest dependent on the Holy Spirit to bring their issues to the light. As they hear the life experience and perspective of the other group members, an opportunity is afforded to them to pursue change. The old axiom is appropriate here. "Unwanted advice is unnecessary criticism". It does not mean that you cannot share your perspective. It does mean that you leave the persuasion up to the Holy Spirit. As a group facilitator, part of your role is to help facilitate that kind of growth atmosphere by keeping the group focused on a safe environment.

o   Summary (Week 9)

This is now the third of four summaries. Most of the group members, if not all, should have a good handle on how this is supposed to work and should have some good personal material to share. Take some time to have individuals in the group share what they have learned to this point. This could involve something they have learned in relationship to Christ, in relationship to self, or in relationship to members in the group. The focus during these "lessons learned" times is on experiential change. As has been stated at the beginning of this journey, this is a life transformation journey. This would also be a good time to highlight briefly ongoing areas where growth is needed. These can become opportunities for prayer and ongoing accountability among the group.

- Fourth Leg Becoming More Wholly Connected with Others, Self, and God Philippians 4 Sections 1-7, Week10-12, Day 24–31

Some of us have a tendency once we get to a certain point in a journey to coast to the end. Encourage group members to finish well by maintaining a passionate commitment to Christ and each other for the remainder being part of this personal and relational transformation journey. In keeping with the overall perspective of the instructions for this journey, the directions are continuing to taper off intentionally. You may want to begin floating the question about potential "next group". As you begin to look toward the conclusion of this three-month journey you will want to solidify gains made on an individual level and on a group level. It might be helpful for you to take the time to record your personal assessment of the growth of individuals and then, the group as a whole. After doing this personally, you might want to spend some time during the remaining group times or have a one- time summary group experience and let each person share their perspective on the group's journey.

o Sections 1-4 (Week 10, Day 24-27)

Listen to the word.

A tool, which has been very helpful for many, is what is called the Feeling Wheel. It is a high chart diagram with core emotions in the center and more specified emotions extending out from each in an ever-widening circle. You can access this online by googling, Feeling Wheel or you can probably get it from one of your church staff members.

Principle #21

As has been mentioned numerous times, if someone has a chronic or nagging core issue that has gone unresolved, it may be advisable to refer them or encourage them to pursue pastoral/professional help. I, of course, do not know how your church culture views seeking pastoral/professional counsel. If, however, you have helped to create an atmosphere in the group that sees it as a strength rather than a weakness, the group members who needed genuinely, will be more open to pursue the assistance that will help unchain them.

Day 25

Read Brief Commentary

This exercise places a much more in-depth focus on Bible study. Although it requires more focus on content, there is a very practical application. What is the practical point? The answer to that question is based on this principle. Give a man a fish. He can eat for a meal. Teach a man to fish. He can eat for a lifetime. Although this exercise goes deeper into Bible study, is not complicated. It does, however, require more effort and digging. Once group members "learn the ropes" they can do their own digging when they have a desire to do so. Doing a word study helps give a more comprehensive perspective on how the word is used. It also provides various shades of meaning that the word can have based on the context.

Day 26

Although there is emphasis on Bible study tools, the ultimate goals are character and life change. How do you keep the group focused on these? How do you stay focused on character and life change rather than getting bogged down in content?

Day 27

Why all the Bible research activities? Part of the purpose of this journey has been to equip each member to better nourish himself or herself. We have tried to provide more tools. FYI-There are even more tools in appendix E Basic Biblical Resources.

o   Sections 5-7 (Week 11, Day 28-30)

Day 28

More tools. Thought visual metaphors are powerful tools. Maybe it would help group members crystallize the practical nature of addressing their thought lives by doing a brainstorming session (no pun intended) in which they come up with mental pictures for the "good-thinking" traits listed in Philippians 4:8, 9. Example 1: true – picture yourself doing your taxes with all accurate truthful information. Example 2: virtuous picture yourself late at night on your computer feeling tempted to view porno and then remembering this verse.

o   Summary (Week 12, Day 31)

Plan on having a celebration during the last group meeting. Take time to rehearse the most significant experiences, lessons learned, ongoing challenges, and plans.

Notes:

Group Covenant Foundation

The group covenant provides healthy boundaries and parameters for which the members commit to the mutual pursuit of personal and relational transformation in Christ. The practicality of having a group covenant is evident in that it provides clarity about the extent and limit of confidentiality. It helps provide the members a way for creating a positive, grace giving, affirming, honest, and safe atmosphere in which to grow in personal transformation.

Part of growth in personal transformation is acknowledging our shortcomings, foibles, faults, misunderstandings, and such. To do this, it requires a certain level of comfort with vulnerability. The individual member's commitment to the group covenant helps to ensure this by providing the safe atmosphere for doing so. It is important for the group leader/facilitator to have a clear understanding of this and a firm commitment to this foundational principle to be able to respond to questions and reservations group members may have. If a safe atmosphere cannot be maintained it will seriously affect the quality of relationships and the progress of the group.

It is recommended that the group itself collectively decide on the group covenant. This will contribute greatly to ownership by group members. The sample group covenant can be used, as it is, if it is adopted as a collaborative decision. You may want to adjust specific wording, but the overall principles should not be changed as they are critical for healthy group interaction and development. The most important concept concerning group covenant is that you are trying to do everything possible to create a group in which all the members have the maximum "buy-in" for the journey. If you do not build this from the beginning the growth and development of the group may be stunted. This is a critical piece of the transformational success of the group.

It is a good idea, but not a requirement, that a special time be designated for the signing of the group covenant. One way of doing this could be to fully explain it and allow time for questions during the introductory session. Then, you would allow time for the potential members to pray over it and discuss it with spouse or significant other. This would also allow those to leave who, for whatever reason, could not commit to participate at this time. Those who had committed to participate would then be re-gathered for a Group Covenant signing and celebration of a new start. You could also hand out the Philippians: A Journey of Personal and Relational Transformation guide.

Group Covenant Worksheet

- Safety (Write out your questions, ideas, reservations, and thoughts concerning this principle. Discuss these and others with your trainer).

- Affirmation-Same

- Positive accountability-Same

- Grace-Same

- Honesty-Same

- Commitment-Same

- Investment-Same

Group Covenant

I _____covenant together with the members of this group to pursue personal and relational transformation in Christ through: Philippians – A Journey of Personal and Relational Transformation. I understand that this journey will be for 12 weeks not including the introductory session. I commit to investing the time, effort, and personal involvement within the context of the group to pursue personal transformation.

Depending upon Christ for the strength and ability to fulfill this covenant, I will seek to be as honest, transparent, and personally accountable. To the extent that I feel safe, I will seek to encourage an atmosphere of safety, grace, and affirmation for the other group members regardless of personality differences.

In a group of this type, it is my understanding that I will be challenged, beyond the level of my comfort zone, but that I will not be pressed to go beyond my readiness. It is my intention that I will seek to grow beyond my comfort zone in pursuing transformation in Christ. It is my purpose to give grace to my fellow group members as they pursue this same purpose.

I will seek to fully support the principles of safety, affirmation, positive accountability, grace giving, honesty, vulnerability, investment, and commitment. If I ever come to the place where I feel as though I cannot fully support these principles, I will willingly remove myself from the group after interacting with the group about it.

Signed _____Date_____

Witness _____Date_____

Appendix C – One Another Passages for Group Relational Development

"One-anothering" in Christ

Romans	12:5	Belong to one another*.
	12:10	Be devoted to one another.
	12:10	Honor one another.
	12:16	Live in harmony with one another.
	12:18	Live at peace with one another*.
	15:7	Accept one another.
1 Corinthians	1:10	Agree with one another.
	10:24	Look out for one another*.
	12:25	Have equal concern for one another*.
	16:20	Greet one another with a holy kiss.
Galatians	5:13	Serve one another.
	6:1	Carry one another's burdens*.
Ephesians	4:2	Bear with one another*.
	4:25	Speak truthfully with one another*.
	4:32	Be kind to one another.
	4:32	Be compassionate to one another.
	4:32	Forgive one another.
	5:19	Speak to one another with psalms, hymns and spiritual songs
	5:21	Submit to one another.
Philippians	2:4	Look to the interests of one another*.
Colossians	3:13	Bear with one another*.
	3:13	Forgive one another.
	3:16	Teach one another.

	3:16	Admonish one another.
1 Thessalonians	4:9	Love one another*.
	4:18	Encourage one another*.
	5:11	Encourage one another.
	5:11	Build up one another*
	5:13	Live in peace with one another*
	5:15	Be kind to one another*
Hebrews	10:24	Spur on one another.
	10:25	Meet with one another*
	10:25	Encourage one another.
	13:1	Love one another*.
James	5:16	Confess your sins to one another*.
	5:16	Pray for one another*.
1 Peter	1:22	Love one another.
	3:8	Live in harmony with one another.
	4:9	Offer hospitality to one another.
	5:14	Greet one another with a kiss of love.
1 John	1:7	Have fellowship with one another.
	3:11	Love one another.
	3:16	Lay down your lives for one another*.
	3:23	Love one another.
	4:7	Love one another.
2 John	5	Love one another.
1 Corinthians	4:6	Don't take pride over against one another*.
Galatians	5:15	Don't devour one another*.
	5:26	Don't envy one another*.
	5:26	Don't provoke one another*.
Colossians	3:9	Don't lie to one another*.
James	5:9	Don't grumble against one another*.

*These statements have been changed from "each other" to "one another."[4]

---

[4] Icenogle, G. W. (1993). *Biblical foundations for small group ministry: An integrative approach.* Downers Grove, IL: InterVarsity Press.

Appendix D – Group Life Cycle and Developmental Dynamics

Transformational Factors

Many factors contribute to the success of any group. Many hurdles, if not managed well, can result in the dilution of the effectiveness of the group's journey or may cause its complete demise. Below, I have listed various critical factors in the development of a group that sees its purpose accomplished. These "successful group factors" are adapted from Irvin Yalom's book, The Theory and Practice of Group Psychotherapy. Yes, I know. What are we doing using a psychotherapy book for a Christian Bible study? All truth, in the world, is God's truth. Just because a source is not "Christian", does not mean that it is not useful. In my graduate marriage and family therapy program, I found great resonance with this highly practical volume. Many of the things we have done in life transformational groups in church are very similar to the therapeutic groups Irvin Yalom has conducted for decades. This journey of personal and relational transformation is not therapy. However, many of the therapeutic factors he discusses in this book are just as applicable in applying God's truth to change lives. I offer them by way of suggestions. You can do with them what you wish, but I have found them to be tremendous guideposts for establishing a successful, transformational group.

He lists 11 therapeutic factors. My take on this is that they are transformational factors. This is the list: hope, universality, information, altruism, corrective recapitulation of the primary group, socializing techniques, imitative behavior, interpersonal learning, cohesiveness, catharsis, and existential factors. Admittedly, some of the terms may seem foreign to a Bible study. Remember, that from the beginning, this journey was not depicted as merely a Bible study, but rather as a personal and relational transformational journey. Therefore, it is oriented to maximizing life change for the individual within the context of a transformational group experience.

The first transformational factor is one that, as believers, we should be very familiar with. The first factor is hope. 1 Corinthians 13 lists this as one of the three top qualities of Christian expression faith, hope, love. It is for the hope of Christ's return that we live our lives. In Scripture it is referred to as the blessed hope. Hope is a powerful motivational factor towards seeing transformation take place. Each time one struggling group member hears the story of another who has struggled through an experience here or she is instilled with hope from the other's experience.

Universality is the second transformational factor. Often, in struggling with temptation, we feel isolated, alone, and as though we are the only one experiencing this battle. When we discover that there are many others experiencing similar battles, we experience encouragement and greater determination to persevere. This factor also helps facilitate the move toward interdependence as we realize we are not in this alone and can help each other.

Imparting information is a transformational factor that believers are very familiar with. We are a people of the Book. We are called upon to memorize and meditate on Bible verses. We are encouraged to listen to sermons, watch inspirational videos, participate in marriage retreats, use online Bible resources, and a host of other tools for learning how to live out our Christian lives. Hopefully, the unique difference in this journey is that the information given is experienced and applied.

Altruism is another way of highlighting the importance of the Bible's one another principles. Each of us has been equipped by God to provide something of value and worth for the benefit of others. We are all contributors. There are no little people. Everyone has significance and importance and is needed as part of God's family. I would invite you to review the One another passages listed in appendix C.

The next transformational factor, as listed by Yalom, includes technical language. He refers to this factor as the corrective recapitulation of the primary family group. What this concept suggests, simply put, is this. We each bring to group the sum of our family of origin relationship dynamics. In other words, we will largely play out in group what we have experienced in family. As a group leader, it is important to realize that the individual group members bring "family baggage" with them. We all do. Group is an opportunity, because it is a larger relationship context, to learn new ways of relating with one another. Part of the reason that I have included this factor for the leaders' information is so that you will have a basic understanding, that what may be happening in group has more to do with their family of origin than it does the group itself. Understanding this can be helpful for you to know to help you demonstrate grace for those who may be difficult to deal with.

The socializing technique transformational factor is somewhat akin to the previous one. The uniqueness of this factor is that it is skill-based. For those who have difficulty in close relationship, the group provides a context in which to watch and learn from others who are farther along in their ability to interact with others in more significant and intimate ways.

Imitative behavior as a transformational factor speaks for itself. Paul said it this way, "Be imitators of me as I am of Christ". A very important aspect of a successful group is that it has more mature members modeling Christ likeness for those who are new to Christ. In many groups, there levels of Christian maturity. One of the challenges of the group leader is to discover early who those more mature practicing members are and seek to facilitate a mentoring atmosphere within the context of the group.

"Interpersonal relationships" is a term akin to the biblical concept of discipleship. In the Bible, a disciple was not a student sitting in a desk learning from the teacher in a classroom. A disciple was one who followed the lifestyle of his Rabbi, teacher, master. He sought to experience life change and follow the model of his teacher. We are hardwired for relationship. In practical terms, what that means, is that no person is an island. We do not grow in Christ apart from relationship with others. This too, is a concept that the "one another" passages highlights. We need one another to gain insight, to become more self-aware, to be able to identify our internal emotional state, to learn how to resolve conflicts in healthy ways, and to be able to grow in personal authenticity and integrity.

A corrective emotional experience, as described by Yalom, includes these components: a strong expression of emotion which is interpersonally directed and constitutes a risk taken, a group supportive enough to permit this risk, reality testing, which allows the individual to examine his situation and receive validation from group members, a recognition of inappropriateness in behavior or emotional expression, and the ultimate facilitation of the individual's ability to interact with others more deeply and honestly. In short, this is a huge part of the goal of personal and relational transformation. Again, this journey is not intended to be merely a Bible study in which members gain more knowledge of information. Its design is to have a life transforming encounter with Christ in the context of a supportive and caring community and to be changed.

If you as a group facilitator will seek to establish, monitor, and maintain your group based upon these transformational factors your group will experience significant life change and the group members will grow in greater and greater depths of spiritual maturity in Christ. You will see a greater buy in for the needed practice of disciplines that will help create an atmosphere of genuine community and positive encouragement. It is a great set of guidelines to gauge how your group is progressing. Then, the following will be a guide for the stages of group progression.

Group Life Cycle and Developmental Dynamics

Get acquainted Stage

Purpose

- get to know each member of the group.
- define goals and strategies.

Activities

- provide for a gender time.
- use the word time for one couple or individual to tell their story; each meeting beginning with the leader. (Share transparently, joys, struggles, and strongholds, etc.)
- Have fellowship time; meal before group, cookout, get acquainted games, etc.

Leadership Concerns

- identify or confirm your apprentice.
- set up a regular time of mentoring outside the group.
- go over group stages and multiplication date.
- have apprentice watch you do ministry.
- meet with supervisor and identify team leaders for the group.

Life Groups Logistics

- set meeting time and dates.
- set meeting place or rotation.
- set refreshment schedule.
- determine how to do worship/handle children.
- get phone numbers, addresses, work schedules, etc. for each member.

Share The Vision

- set forth the projected multiplication date the first meeting.
- project vision for outreach and pray for unsaved persons.

Results

- this stage allows the group members to feel comfortable with each other.
- learning the history of another person allows identification with and respect for the person.
- this time allows the leader to assess where each person is spiritually and how comfortable they feel ensuring.

Time Frame

- 4 to 6 meetings depending on size of the group.
- you have reached this stage when people become friends.

Conflict/Congealing Stage Storming

Purpose

- allow the group to become real with each other.
- resolve conflicts which could hinder the group from achieving the broader purpose.

Activities

- identify problem people or antagonists.
- handle these with the help of leadership
- firmly establish the format that
- divide men and women during gender time.
- use tact and sensitivity when dealing with conflict issues (you may want to work at it individually first)
- affirm each person's talents and gifts.
- encourage each person to minister.
- pray for each other.

Leadership Concerns

- encourage apprentice to minister in the group.
- continue to talk with your apprentice about what you did and why.
- meet with your supervisor.
- identify potential apprentices for multiplication.

Life Group Logistics

- make group atmosphere is ministry friendly as possible.

Share The Vision

- continue to lift each person as a minister.
- pray for persons group members have identified for outreach.

Results

- bonding takes place is personal growth happens.
- you have work through conflicts rather than running from them or denying they exist.
- you have referred problems people to a place where they can get help.
- the group is free to enter unhindered ministry.

Time Frame

- 4 to 6 meetings
- you have reached this stage when the cell is at peace and ready to focus on ministry to one another.

Community Stage Norming

Purpose

- to realize the group has developed significant ministry in relationships.
- to minister to the ongoing struggles that life group members have
- to intentionally begin to reach out to others beyond group.

Activities

- continue with the format of the group.
- have an extended night of prayer for the purpose of drawing nearer to God
- encouraging give opportunity for all members to minister to each other.
- pray for each other.

Leadership Concerns

- begin to lead the group with your apprentice.
- give the apprentice parts of the group to lead.
- continue to meet with your apprentice and talk about what you did and why.
- talk about the ministry dynamics within the group.
- give responsibilities to potential apprentices.

Life Group Logistics

- troubleshoot any space problems you might have as a group grows.
- begin praying for new people.

Share The Vision

- pray for opportunities to do outreach.

Results

- the group sees ministry opportunities not only within the group but also outside of it.
- the group focus is beginning to become outward.
- group members feel confident to minister is a Holy Spirit anoints them.

Time Frame

- 4 to 6 meetings
- you have reached this stage when you see members reaching out to others.

Outreach Stage Performing

Purpose

- grow the group through the natural relationships which each group member has developed.
- to minister to one another and beyond the group

Activities

- continue the format of the group.
- minister to ongoing group needs
- prepare group to welcome new members.

Leadership Concerns

- have directions ready for new members so they can find the group.
- incorporate new members into the flow of the life group.
- begin to think about how the group will multiply.

Share The Vision

- group will move in your midst.
- the group will grow.
- the group members will mature as a Holy Spirit's ministry flows through the
- the group will be ready to multiply.

Time Frame

- 8 to 10 meetings
- you have reached the stage when the group grows to an average of 12 in attendance and leadership is developed to give direction to the new group.

Multiplication Stage Transforming

Purpose

- to multiply

Activities

- continue the group format.
- set final multiplication date.
- discern relationship lines and discerning the actual multiplication.
- have communion together at the last group meeting.

Leadership Concerns

- have new leadership teams in place, leader, and apprentice.
- meet with the supervisor.

Life Group Logistics

- begin to work at the details of each new group.

Share The Vision

- pray that the new groups will grow and multiply.

Results

- the group multiplies into new groups.

Time Frame

- 2 to 4 meetings maximum
- you have reached this stage when two healthy groups emerge from one.
- each group then start the cycle over again.

Total Life Group Cycle Time: 22 to 32 meetings (6 to 8 months)

Appendix E – Resources

Group Member Resource

Benner, David. (2009). Opening to God: Lectio Divina.

Carpenter, E. E., & Comfort, P. W. (). Hollman Treasury of Key Bible Words-200 Greek/200Hebrew Words Defined and Explained.

Drane, J. (1999). Introducing the New Testament. Oxford, England: A Lion Book.

Dunnett, W. M. (2001). Exploring the New Testament. Wheaton, Illinois: Crossway Books

Karleen, P. S. (). The Handbook of Bible Study.

McArthur, J. F. (). How to Study the Bible.

McArthur, J. F. (1995). Alone with God: The Power and Passion of Prayer. Wheaton, Illinois: Victor Books.

Neighbour, R. (2004). Community Life 101. Houston, Texas: Cell Group Resources.

Wiersbe, W. (1989). The Bible Expository Commentary. Wheaton, Illinois: Victor Books.

Yerkovick, M., & Yerkovick, K. (2006). How We Love. Colorado Springs, Co:Waterbrook Press

Group Facilitator Resources

Anonymous. (2012). the Twelve Steps: A Spiritual Journey. Scotts Valley, California: RPI Publishing, Inc.

Arnold, J. (2004). The Big Book on Small Groups (2nd ed.). Downers Grove, Illinois: Inter Varsity Press.

Barker, S. (). Good Things Come in Small Groups: The Dynamics of Good Group Life.

Benner, David. (2009). Opening to God: Lectio Divina.

Blanchard, K. & Hodges, P. (2003). The Servant Leader. Nashville, Tn: Thomas Nelson

Carpenter, E. E., & Comfort, P. W. (). Hollman Treasury of Key Bible Words-200 Greek/200Hebrew Words Defined and Explained.

Carter, L. & Minirth, F. (1993). The Anger Workbook. Nashville, Tn: Thomas Nelson.

Drane, J. (1999). Introducing the New Testament. Oxford, England: A Lion Book.

Dunnett, W. M. (2001). Exploring the New Testament. Wheaton, Illinois: Crossway Books

Geisler, N. L., & Nix, W. E. (). A General Introduction to the Bible, Revised and Expanded.

Griffin, E. A. (). Getting Together: A Guide for Good Groups.

Hastings, J. (Ed.). (1915). The Christian Doctrine of Prayer. Edinburgh: T and T Clark.

Icenogle, G. W. (1994). Biblical Foundations for Small Group Ministry. Downers Grove, Illinois: Intervarsity Press.

Karleen, P. S. (). The Handbook of Bible Study.

Laaser, M. (2008). L.I.F.E. Guide for Men. Lake Mary, Florida: L.I.F.E. Ministries International.

MacArthur, J. F. (1996). Different by Design. Wheaton, Illinois: Victor Books.

MacArthur, J. F. (). How to Study the Bible.

MacArthur, J. F. (1995). Alone with God: The Power and Passion of Prayer. Wheaton, Illinois: Victor Books.

McNeal, R. (2006). Practicing Greatness:7 Disciplines of Extraordinary Spiritual Leaders. San Francisco, Ca: Jossey Bass.

Myra, H. (). 1999. Waco, Texas: Word Books Publisher.

Neighbor, R. (2004). Community Life 101. Houston, Texas:Cell Group Resources

Osbeck, K. W. (1999). 366 Inspiring Hymn Stories for Daily Devotions. Grand Rapids, MI: Kregel Publications.

Schaumburg, H. W. (1992). False Intimacy: Understanding the Struggle of Sexual Addiction. Colorado Springs, Co: Navpress.

Swanson, J. (2001). A Dictionary of Biblical Languages: Greek New Testament (2nd ed.). [Logos Research Systems]. Retrieved from http://www.logosbiblesoftware.com

Thiessen, H. C. (). Great Doctrines of the Bible: Vol. 1 God the Father and the Son.

Thiessen, H. C. (2000). Anthropology. In Lectures in Systematic Theology (p. 181). Grand Rapids, Mi: Wm B. Eerdmans.

Wiersbe, W. (1989). The Bible Expository Commentary. Wheaton, Illinois: Victor Books.

Yalom, I. D., & Leszcz, M. (2005). The Theory and Practice of Group Psychotherapy (5th ed.). New York: Basic Books.

Yerkovick, M., & Yerkovick, K. (2006). How We Love. Colorado Springs, Co:Waterbrook Press.

Appendix F – Worship Resources Per Day

This worship appendix is provided so that you may have a ready reference to your favorate genre of worship music and "message through music" that is relevant to each day's meditation. This is provided to enrich a more full, more impactful experience of your intimate time with God. We hope your time with God does become a rich, treasured, and cherished time that you lean heavily on daily. Then, watch your transformation progress.

Day 1-Introduction to the Journey

1. Hymn: How Firm a Foundation
2. Let Your Glory Shine - Lincoln Brewster
3. Today Is the Day - Lincoln Brewster

Day 2-Becoming More Authentic and Self-Aware

1. Hymn: A Mighty Fortress - Martin Luther
2. The Power of Your Name - Lincoln Brewster
3. Who You Say I Am - Hillsong Worship

Day 3-Passionate Prayer

1. Hymn: Sweet Hour of Prayer
2. There Is None Like You – Michael W. Smith
3. Open the Eyes of My Heart Piano Instrumental – David Carnes

Day 4-Confidence in God's Work

1. Hymn: My Redeemer Lives – Fanny Cosby
2. Salvation Is Here – Lincoln Brewster
3. Who You Say I Am – Hillsong Worship

Day 5-Passionate Support for One Another

1. Hymn: Everlasting Love
2. The Arms of the Savior – Lincoln Brewster
3. Your Love Is Enough – Jon Foreman

Day 6-Authentic Expanding Excellent Love

1. Hymn: Jesus Loves Me, This I Know
2. Reckless Love – Cory Asbury
3. How He Loves Me – Crowder Band

Day 7-Suffering Triumphantly

1. Hymn: Onward Christian Soldier
2. Dancing In the Rain - K.J.
3. Even If - Kutless

Day 8-Serving Christ by Serving Others, My Highest Joy

1. Hymn: The Solid Rock
2. In Christ Alone - Your favorite artist
3. Let Your Glory Shine – Lincoln Brewster

Day 9-Lives Lived Worthy of the Gospel of Christ

1. Hymn: Our Great Savior – J. Wilbur Chapman
2. Salvation Is Here – Lincoln Brewster
3. He Is – Crowder Band

Day 10- Leg 1 Summary of Transformation Principles

1. Extended Time of Worship with Favorite Worship Songs
2. "   "   "   "   "   "   "   "   "   "
3.   "   "   "   "   "   "   "   "   "

Day 11-Emulate the Humility of Christ

1. Hymn: Love Divine All Loves Excelling – Charles Wesley
2. How He Loves You and Me – Kurt Kaiser
3. How He Loves – Crowder Band – Live from Passion

Day 12-Leave Promotion to God and Seek to Serve

1. Hymn: The Solid Rock: My Hope Is Built on Nothing Less
2. He Is Lord – Based of Philippians 2:10,11
3. What a Beautiful Name – Hillsong Worship

Day 13-Working Out What God Has Implanted

1. Hymn: How Firm a Foundation
2. He Is Exalted – Twila Paris
3. Again, I Say Rejoice – Israel Houghton

Day 14-Model Humble Servanthood

1. Hymn: Make Me a Servant – Kelly Woodward or your favorite artist
2. Goodness Of God – Gospel Praise and Worship
3. I Offer My Life to You

Day 15-Model Self-sacrifice for Others Serving Christ

1. Hymn: Man of Sorrows – Phillip P. Bliss
2. The Anchor – Crowder Band
3. Something About the Name – Kirk Franklin

Day 16-Leg 2 Summary of Transformation Principles

1. Extended Time of Worship with Favorite Worship Songs
2. "   "   "   "   "   "   "   "   "
3. "   "   "   "   "   "   "   "   "

Day 17-Rely Solely on the Righteousness of Christ

1. Hymn: On Christ the Solid Rock
2. He Is – Crowder Band
3. Turn Your Eyes upon Jesus – Michael W. Smith

Day 18-Christ Over All

1. Hymn: All Hail the Power of Jesus Name
2. All Hail King Jesus – Steffany Gretzinger – Bethel Worship Music
3. Warrior of Heaven -Gospel Worship

Day 19-Release Self-righteousness for God's Righteousness

1. Hymn: When I Survey the Wondrous Cross – Isaac Watts
2. Break Every Chain – Cece Winans
3. Prayin' for You – Lecrae music video

Day 20-Passion to Know Christ Experientially

1. Hymn: I Want to Be Like Jesus – Thomas O. Chisolm
2. Draw Me Close to You – The Katinas
3. Everything I Need - Kutless

Day 21-Lifelong Pursuit of Christ

1. Hym: Fairest Lord Jesus -Anonymous
2. It is Well – A Worship Album by Kutless
3. Jesus, I Need You – Hillsong Worship

Day 22-Keeping our Eyes on Jesus

1. Hymn: The Old Rugged Cross – George Berman
2. Strong Tower - Kutless
3. The Cross of Christ – Passion – Chris Tomlin

Day 23-Leg 3 – Summary of Transformation Principles

1. Extended Time of Worship and Favorite Worship Songs-Celebration
2. "   "   "   "   "   "   "   "   "-Contemplation
3. "   "   "   "   "   "   "   "   "-Reflection

Day 24-A Solid Unified Team

1. Hymn: The Church's One Foundation – Rev. Samuel John Stone
2. You Say-Lauren Daigle
3. In Christ Alone (My Hope is Found) – Adrienne Liesching-Hadleigh Baptist Church

Day 25-Live a Lifestyle of Joy

1. Hymn: Jesus, Joy of Our Desiring - Bach
2. This is the Day (Reimagined)- Lakewood Music
3. Rejoice in the Lord (a-cappella) -The Hamilton Family – Majestic Music

Day 26-Living Gentle as Jesus

1. Hymn: Pass Me Not, O Gentle Savior – Fernando Ortega
2. I Surrender – Hillsong Worship
3. The Lion and the Lamb – Big Daddy Weave

Day 27-Stop Worrying, Start Praying, Experience Peace

1. Hymn: Prince of Peace Worship Sequence – "Let's Worship and Adore Him, I Extol You, O Come All Ye Faithful"
2. I Surrender – Hillsong Worship
3. Jesus – Chris Tomlin

Day 28-Meditating on the Things That Bring Life

1. Hymn: How Great Thou Art – Stuart K. Hine
2. Alone With God: 3 Hour Worship Music for Prayer and Meditation – Dappy T. Keys
3. One Hour of Praise and Worship on Piano: 17 Contemporary Songs- Kaleb Braisee

Day 29-Contentment in Christ

1. Hymn: Victory in Jesus - Eugene M. Barlett
2. It is Well – Austin Stone Worship Live
3. Firm Foundation – Maverick City and Elevation Worship

Day 30-

1. Hymn: Be Thou My Vision – Mary E. Byrne
2. Jireh – Elevation Worship and Maverick City
3. It is Well – Kritiene DeMarco – Bethel Music

Day 31- Final – Summary of Transformation Principles

1. Extended Time of Worship and Favorite Worship Songs-Celebration
2.   "   "   "   "   "   "   "   "-Contemplation
3.   "   "   "   "   "   "   "   "-Reflection

Appendix G – Frequently Asked Questions- To be added based on feedback and questions from training sessions.

Appendix G – Staff Support - to be added per church staff.

Printed in the United States
by Baker & Taylor Publisher Services